THE SKY'S THE LIMIT

LESSONS LEARNED IN THE COCKPIT

JIM STOCKDALE

THE SKY'S THE LIMIT

Copyright © 2020 by James M Stockdale, Jr

FIRST EDITION

ISBN: 978-1-7338956-4-4

For more information, about this book or others written by
Jim Stockdale contact: jim@latinamericanministry.org or
laministry@yahoo.com

www.LatinAmericanMinistry.org

This book is dedicated to the man who,
taught me to fly and asked nothing in return - Captain Richard
Lonell Price (Rick) - Flight Safety, Wichita, KS, and
eighteen year NetJets Captain (Retired)

TABLE OF CONTENTS

ACKNOWLEDGEMENTS

The list of people to whom I owe thanks for this book is a long one. I will endeavor to be short winded to redeem the time, but to fail to recognize these people would be worse than to be longwinded.

Pam Stockdale - Who but you? When but then? 1980 was my best year on earth. It's the year we began our flight together. You're love and partnership for forty years has been the constant in my life and it is beyond description. Thank you for saying yes and always pushing me to be more. Your readers only read what you write. I get to know the writer and am infinitely better because of you. I'm blessed to be your husband.

Ray Harkey - Meeting you at the CAP meeting in May of 2003 was an intricate part of my flying future. You have been a friend, flying mentor and ministry partner since that time. Thank you for the Bi-Annual Flight Reviews donated. Since 2004 it has been your single minded purpose to provide "in-cockpit weather" to us and that gift has no doubt made many flights possible that would have otherwise been impossible. When very few single engine airplanes had Nexrad Weather Radar, N30230 had it. Thank you friend.

Danny Dubose - It is unfortunate that all those who will read this book aren't privileged to know you personally. Bama Air will forever be a part of my memory and history. Thank you for providing both equipment and funding to help us accomplish the dream. It was you who introduced me to Mike Poindexter and flying in Mexico. I learned to fly in airplanes that you owned. Thank you.

Mike Poindexter - Many of the experiences written in the following pages occurred because of our friendship. While you didn't teach me to fly, you taught me how to do so in Mexico and to do it safely. Perhaps you saved our lives without even knowing it. I had 75 total time hours when Pam and I flew to Weslaco, TX to go to Durango, MX with you. I shall never forget my experiences with you in the Sierra Madre's. Above all, thank you for introducing me to John Hudson.

Doug & Judy Vaubel - At a missions conference in Cold Water, AL, in 2004, Judy stopped at our booth and asked Pam the question, "What do you do with an airplane in missions? My husband is an airplane mechanic and is looking for a way to be involved in missions." From that encounter

Doug became our first A & P, and AI. It seems too small, but thank you to both of you for getting us through those early years of tight budgets and uncertain times.

John & Cheryl Hudson, Grace Aviation, & 2nd Baptist Church Kingstree, SC - Your partnership with LAM has sustained us for many years. For more than 15 years you have been our A & P, AI and friends. Thank you for keeping us flying through your professionalism and expertise. The list is long of tireless work you have performed. From engine to interior N30230 has had great care from you two and the volunteers at Grace Aviation. Thank you.

Rick Price - I can't tell it all here. This list of acknowledgements would be incomplete without your name on it. When I started down this road, you were not my friend but my instructor. Somewhere early along that journey you moved into another category, that of friend. Since that day in the lobby of Daystar Family Church in 2002 we have been working toward the same thing, winning people for Christ and making disciples. My respect for you as an instructor will become obvious to everyone who reads this book. It was your wisdom and teaching that kept me from killing myself and/or someone else along the way. You donated your instruction time. All I bought was the gas. I've heard it said, "You get what you pay for." I usually agree with that statement, but in this case it's untrue. I paid nothing but received everything. You gave everything and received nothing. Until you're better paid, thank you Rick. I'm forever in your debt for the gift of flight. Let's log more time together in the air.

Jonathan Anglin - Thank you for giving me the title of this book. You read the introduction and first chapter and then suggested the title to me. I used your suggestion and am glad I did. I promised you a copy and I will deliver.

To our many LAM Partners - It has been your spiritual, prayerful and financial support that has made this flight and book possible. Thank you.

ENDORSEMENTS

"A great read, especially for pilots, but applies to EVERYONE looking to seek and follow the course God's planned and mapped out for their life's journey."

Ronnie Barton, *CEO, Roll Haulers, Private Pilot*

In May of 2003, a newly minted private pilot named Jim Stockdale and flight instructor, Rick Price attended a Civil Air Patrol meeting in Tuscaloosa, AL. Rick had suggested that Jim check out the CAP to further his flight training. It was a divine appointment for both of us since I am a pilot, an instructor pilot, a check pilot, and most importantly a fellow brother in Christ. We have become best of friends and flown together many times, including several mission to Mexico. Jim is an excellent pilot and tremendous preacher and writer. As an instructor I recommend The Sky's The Limit. It is an excellent read for pilots and non-pilots alike. It will point you to "higher heights!"

Ray Harkey, *CFI, CFII, MEI*

The Sky's The Limit is an amazing book that will encourage and equip you with faith filled nuggets of how God can inspire, challenge, teach and sometimes humble us thru His process in our life. We all have desires, dreams and ambitions for our own lives, but God also has a plan and purpose, this is called The Process. Thru this book Jim has a unique way of comparing his experience of learning how to fly an airplane with his experience of learning how to lean on and follow Jesus. Get the book, enjoy the journey.

Danny DuBose, *Director of Flight Operations*
- The University of Alabama (Retired)
Former owner of Bama Air Inc,
Tuscaloosa, AL (FBO), Commercial Pilot

I met Jim Stockdale over 16 years ago when he landed in Weslaco Texas on his way to a mission project he was working on in Mexico. I liked what I saw and the vision he and his wife Pam had. I knew that it would take years to accomplish. Yet, I wanted my operation to be a part of this endeavor to reach the lost and unchurched with the message of Jesus Christ. WOW, how the years have flown by. (Pardon the pun) For over 15 years we have been partnering with Jim and Pam by servicing their aircraft annually and providing aviation technical support. I am thrilled to see the creation of the book you hold. It contains some of the adventures of one of the finest ministering couples I have ever known. Whether you're a pilot or not, read and relax. Enjoy what

God has been doing and what He can do for anyone who steps out in faith, trusting HIM. There are lessons here to be learned here. I suggest a highlighter.

John M Hudson, Director of Grace Aviation NDMI
FAA A/P & Airworthiness Inspector
Retired Southern Baptist Pastor, 40 Years

FOREWORD

He was a stranger to me, though his name had been mentioned one day by a friend from Daystar Family Church. Jim Stockdale was calling to ask if I would be his flight instructor. As we talked on the phone that summer afternoon I had no idea that all the cosmic tumblers were moving into their God-ordained position to open wide a giant door that would lead to the next vital step in Jim's divinely orchestrated call to missions in Latin America, and in the World. That moment in time was a "God moment," and I was a part of it.

Along the way, Jim and I would begin writing our story of a lifelong friendship that is still being penned at this moment. During nearly two decades as "the best of friends," we have walked together through many seasons of life and experienced the mountaintops and valleys that always accompany those seasons. I am an airline transport pilot with seventeen thousand hours of flight experience. I have flown more than four million miles over a 45-year flight career. My travels have taken me from the sub-zero temperatures of Northern Canada to the blistering temperatures of Tobago and Trinidad, and to a whole lot of destinations, with passengers or freight, at seemingly every airport large and small between the two places.

Jim Stockdale's passion for flying revealed itself early and often during his flight training. His hunger to learn made him an exceptional student. His passion molded him into a skillful and experienced pilot whom I would trust to fly my family anywhere and anytime. He has been to airports which could only be described as the side of a mountain, where rough and rugged grass strips provide limited services to isolated groups of Mexico's mountain communities. He has also traversed some of the busiest airports in and around our largest cities in America. I personally think he may hold the record among pilots for the most miles and trips to Mexico in the same single engine fixed gear airplane for ministry purposes.

Jim and I have spent countless hours exploring the backroads of Alabama on motorcycles. We have "made waves" on the Ross Barnette Reservoir on jet skis, and broken bread together more times than I can count around a fire-pit in his backyard, where good food, laughter, and hospitality became a refreshing refuge for anyone and everyone who could find their way to their patio. We have flown as a flight crew in the "Wings of Hope" Piper Archer II, from Tuscaloosa, Alabama to Saltillo, Mexico, to provide support for feeding centers which sometimes reach 100 children in a single day. They are the toddlers and teens who are known to many as Mexico's "forgotten children of the street." Jim Stockdale is the guy I want by my side if I ever find myself in a foxhole in the middle of a war zone in some far away land. He is the guy I will call when the odds are stacked against me and I need a friend or an advocate.

Jim actually began his personal, "The Sky's the Limit" journey as a teenager, when he answered God's call to full time ministry. Since that life-changing milestone, he has populated each mile-marker of his life with monuments in the shape of "changed lives" from every walk of life. The fusion of family and friends is inspired by a man who has influenced cowboys and construction workers, musicians and millworkers to live the best life, one that is forged on the anvil of prayer and obedience to the creator of this universe. In this book, Jim paints a portrait, in vivid color, of everyday life where you live, and on the flight-deck that merge and mirror each other like a pouch full of shimmering diamonds spilled out on a black velvet display cloth.

After reading this manuscript four times, I find myself drawn back to its pages by some magnetic force again and again to marinate my mind and soul in another one of the principles that leap out at me in every chapter. These simple concepts, with profound impact, are woven together like a magnificent tapestry of experience, knowledge, and faith, revealing the supernatural power and authority we have to become more than we are today. Jim offers up to us a new flight plan, not of this world, that will change the course and destiny of your life. Whoever you are, wherever you are living life today, this book will be the catalyst to move you from the last seat in the back of the plane, where you are just along for the ride, to your God-ordained place on the flight-deck. You will be energized to take the "controls of your life" and begin to climb in the direction of new hopes and dreams. Your thought process will ascend into positive airspace and your actions will maneuver you into a new place where you will take ownership of a life where, The Sky's The Limit.

Richard Lonell Price
ATP/CFII/MEI
MU300CE-560XL/BE400/LR-45

GLOSSARY OF TERMS

I realize that many who will read this book are perhaps aviators both as a profession and/or a hobby. For you, these words are common, however, for the non-aviator I've included a short glossary of terms and words you'll hear in this book:

- **Controls or yoke** - What in layman's terms appears to be a steering wheel.

- **Knots** - A nautical term used to indicate speed. A knot is 1.15 MPH

- **Rudder** - A fin located on the horizontal stabilizer which controls movement around the vertical axis, much like the rudder of a boat or ship.

- **Ailerons** - These are the moving airfoils located on the ends of each wing and control lateral movement.

- **Windscreen** - Windshield

- **Panel** - The dashboard in an airplane.

- **Airspeed Indicator** - Speedometer

- **Attitude Indicator** - A vacuum operated gyro that indicates whether the airplane is climbing, descending, or turning left or right. (Sometimes called an artificial horizon)

- **Altimeter** - An instrument displaying the altitude of the airplane.

- **Turn Coordinator** - An electric gyro which displays the coordination of the rudder and the ailerons.

- **Inclinometer** - A part of the turn coordinator which demonstrates yaw. (Side to side movement of the airplane)

- **Mixture** - The air/gas mix in an airplane.

- **Carburetor Heat** - This provides heat from the engine to the carburetor to avoid ice build ups that can occur in normally aspirated engines.

- **MSL** - Mean Sea Level - Obstructions are given in MSL (i.e. towers, mountains, buildings, etc.)

- **AGL** - Above Ground Level - Cloud coverage is given in AGL.

- **Hold line** - The line drawn across a taxi way that marks the beginning of the runway. The hold line may not be crossed at a controlled airport until the Control Tower has cleared the traffic to do so.

- **Traffic pattern** - The flow of air traffic around an airport runway. (See diagram)

- **Upwind leg**- This is the departure leg of a traffic pattern at an airport.

- **Crosswind leg** - This refers the first 90° turn in a traffic pattern.

- **Downwind leg**- The part of a traffic pattern which is adjacent to the runway.

- **Base leg** - The second 90° turn in a traffic pattern and ends with a left turn to final approach.

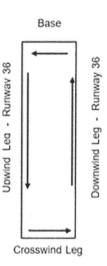

- **Final approach** - The third 90° turn in a traffic pattern that ends at the runway.

- **Ramp** - The area where airplanes are parked and movement is allowed without a clearance.

- **FBO** - Fixed Base of Operations is what laymen would call the terminal area in a small airport. It's where gas is purchased, flight plans are made and passengers are picked up and dropped off.

- **Pilotage** - The ability to identify objects and/or waypoints on the ground, from the air.

- **Dead Reckoning** - The term is taken from "Deduced Reckoning." It is not an abbreviation of "deduced" as supposed but meant to convey something being "fixed" or dead ahead. It is the ability to navigate from a known position to another waypoint using a set of known or assumed qualities such as: A compass, wind speed and direction, and vehicle speed. It was the navigation method used by Maritime captains for centuries.

- **PIC** - Pilot in command

- **VOR** - VHF Omnidirectional Radio is a radio signal being broadcast from a fixed point with a 360 degree tracking ability for aircraft.

- **FAA** - Federal Aviation Administration

- **POH** - Pilot's Operating Handbook is a document developed by the airplane manufacturer and contains the FAA approved Airplane Flight Manual information.

- **IMC** - Instrument Meterological Conditions

- **IFC** - Instrument Meterological Conditions

- **IFR** - Instrument Flight Rules

- **VFR** - Instrument Flight Rules

- **MDA** - Minimum descent altitude

- **IAF** - Initial approach fix

- **FAF** - Final approach fix

- **Approach plate** - Approach plates are the printed charts of instrument approach procedures that pilots use to fly instrument approaches during instrument flight rules (IFR) operations. (Wikipedia)

INTRODUCTION

As the door on the Cessna 172 closed, I caught the unfamiliar smell of avionics, vinyl, cloth, and old carpet. It was a smell that I would come to both recognize and look forward to. Per his instructions, I sat in the left seat and hooked my seatbelt, as my instructor, Rick Price, flipped switches and made unknown adjustments. Soon, I was asked to turn the key in the ignition switch and watched as the propeller began to turn. As the engine roared into life, so did my heart. It seemed it was turning as fast as the propeller. I knew that, somehow, this new chapter in my life would be one that I was destined to write and I was eager to begin. It wasn't without trepidation however, if it hadn't been for the comforting assurance coming from Rick, and the knowledge that other students had sat where I was sitting, I would certainly have bolted from the cockpit of that little airplane, but I sat firm and awaited instructions, thinking I would only be an observer on this introductory flight.

With headsets in place and wind from the propeller cooling the small cockpit on that hot August day in Tuscaloosa, AL, Rick called ground control on the radio and received taxi instructions to runway 22. Sitting quietly in the pilot's seat, and much to my surprise, I heard Rick say, "Take the controls, put your feet on the pedals to steer the plane and taxi where I tell you." Suddenly I was aware that he had placed me in the pilot's seat not as an observer, but as a participant. I was ok with that as long as he was giving the instructions and overseeing my compliance.

Unless you are a pilot, you may not know that while on the ground airplanes are steered using your feet, not your hands. Although I knew this to be true before that day, doing so was something completely new to me. It felt odd to be using my feet to do what I had always used my hands to do while driving. With me pushing the pedals to turn left and right, we taxied to what I would soon learn was called the "hold line" of runway 22. The hold line is a set of hashed and solid yellow lines, painted across the taxiway, which are illegal to cross without a clearance from tower or ground control. Once there, we began going through a series of preflight confirmations called a check list. It was the same list Rick had used before starting the engine. The little airplane rocked and shook as the RPMs were advanced in order to check the left and right magnetos and carburetor heat. With power reduced and the check list completed, I listened as Rick now spoke on yet another radio frequency called, "Tuscaloosa Tower." The tower controller responded with instructions, "N6545D hold short runway 22." Moments later I heard the same voice say, "N6545D, cleared for takeoff runway 22, climb maintain 2000 feet, report four miles west of the field."

I learned many lessons in the cockpit of that little airplane, and in others I have flown since. In this book we will discuss many of those lessons. Most importantly you will discover that this flight you're on called "life" is not meant to be completed alone. You are not called to be an observer but rather a participant. You have an instructor sitting in the seat beside you. It is He who will give you directions for the many decisions you will have to make in order to complete this journey, but it is you who will fly the plane. Listen carefully and often for His instructions and you won't become lost or dashed on the rocks below. You will soar to new heights and feel His strong hands on the controls with yours while navigating the difficult wind gusts and situations which will arise.

From the very first flight with my instructor to the check ride with my examiner, I was a sponge. I was looking for every possible solution to uncomfortable situations which flying exposed me to. These were the beginning days of feeling the three axes of movement, meaning that I was in a vessel that moved along a straight line, turned left and right, climbed, and descended. Three-axis movement was a new experience for me. There were times of sheer terror and other times of pure ecstasy as I learned the lessons I am about to share with you. I hope you find the same pleasure in reading this work as I had in acquiring the knowledge shared in it. Read on to discover what I found to be true: The sky really is the limit and each mile is worth the investment.

The small cockpit of an airplane is a big classroom. I learned that even though there is a law of gravity which demands respect, there is another law which supersedes it: The law of lift. I learned that fear can only control you if you allow it to speak louder than your dream. Thirdly, I learned that even though you can't see your destination against the vast horizon stretching before you, if you stay the course and trust your compass you will eventually get where you're going. I will share these and many other cockpit lessons in the following pages, so come along, buckle up and join me for a ride into the wild blue yonder in this book I've entitled The Sky's The Limit.

Jim Stockdale

CHAPTER 1

LEARNING THE PROCESS

With the clearance from Tuscaloosa Tower still reverberating in our headsets, I knew the moment of truth had come. We crossed the hold line and turned to point the nose of the airplane down the runway. I watched as Rick advanced the red knob already identified to me as the throttle. With it in the full forward position or "fire-walled," I looked down the runway and anticipated the feeling of flight.

Having been a fan of airplanes and flight for most of my life, I was ready for this moment. It had been long in coming and to best describe it, allow me to digress a moment. The year was late 1999 or early 2000 and we were still pastoring a church in Pierre, South Dakota. We were hosting a special guest one weekend and during that service he stopped and said, "Have you been praying for an airplane?" As I had been, I answered, "Yes!" He then proceeded to tell the congregation that the Lord had instructed him to receive an offering to go toward its purchase and flight training. I remember this so clearly, because he also gave a check

5

in that offering and I watched as his check, folded into a small airplane, came sailing to the altar. I never forgot that day.

Later, while driving to work in Tuscaloosa, AL and with those memories safely tucked away in the back corner of my mind, I clearly heard the Holy Spirit whisper to me, "Did you believe all those words you received about flying, and that you're gonna own an airplane?" I quickly responded, "Yes I did!" With a similar lack of hesitancy from Him I heard, "Don't you think you ought to learn to fly one?" With that I went to my office at the church where I was working as worship pastor, and called the man whom I had met only once but whose wife and daughter were in the choir and worship team. I asked him an unfair but honest question. "Would you consider donating flight lessons to me?" His reply was just as honest, "Let me pray about it." That was how my connection with Rick Price began. I called and asked for free flight lessons. Who would be so bold? Me! There were a few things I knew:

- I had a mandate from God to learn to fly.
- I couldn't afford the full price at the time.
- If this was really God speaking to me, He was going to make it possible for me.

Rick didn't call me back that day but he did very soon and his answer was "Yes I will, but I will need to re-certify my instructor's license. If you will pay for that, I will teach you for free." I agreed, and within a few days we were picking up speed on runway 22 in that little Cessna 172.

As the main landing gear on N6545D left the ground, I remember watching the wheels stop turning. I watched as Rick turned knobs, flipped switches, and rolled the trim wheel adjusting the nose of the airplane with one hand, all the while holding the controls with the other and talking on the radio using aviation language which I couldn't understand. I can tell you today that I wasn't the least bit scared of that flight, but if I could have got out of that airplane at that moment I would have never looked back. I had a moment of anxiety in which I distinctly remember thinking, "There's no way I could ever do this alone." Have you ever felt like the thing that God has promised you is too much, it's just too big, it's over my head and I'm just not equal to the task? If so, you're in good company.

The bible is full of people who were afraid, and had to be reminded of who their God was. Even many of those we revere as great men of faith today had their moments when faith looked small. Think about Gideon, the man we remember as a great warrior and who was responsible for breaking a long period of oppression from the Midianites. Even he, when first visited by an angel, was in hiding and using a wine press to conceal the fact that he was really threshing wheat. When the angel of the Lord appeared to Gideon, he said, "The Lord is with you, you mighty man of valor!" Judges 6:12 *NKJV*

---

*The presence of fear is not a disqualifier
for the presence of God.*

If fear disqualifies us, then God has a lot of explaining to do about why He still used Abraham, Moses, Gideon, Elijah, and the disciples—and the list continues. The counter balance to fear is faith: 1 John 4:8 assures us that "…Perfect love casts out all fear." So here's the point: How do you cast out something that's not there in the first place? You can't. John was encouraging us to trust in the perfected love of Jesus in order to deal with the fears in our life, so that we can continue to do the things we're called to do even in the presence of a perceived fear to do so.

With that knowledge firmly seated in my mind and heart, I released that fear, and with confidence I trusted in my instructor's ability to teach me how to do everything he was doing, even when the time came for me to be in the cockpit alone. Jesus said to His disciples, "Most assuredly, I say to you, he who believes in Me, the works that I do he will do also; and greater works than these he will do, because I go to My Father." John 14:12 *NKJV*

I knew that by the time I had completed all the necessary steps to solo, I would be both confident and competent to do so. Your instructor will never call upon you to do something you're incapable of. "God, who called you to become his child, will do all this for you, just as he promised." 1 Thessalonians 5:22 (*The*

Message) If you're unsure of the one who has called you, you will be unsure of what He can do through you. Conversely, once you know the power of the one who has called you, nothing and nobody can stop you from reaching the plan and purpose He has for you. *The Sky's The Limit* if you know who's providing the lift.

Can You Save Us?

As the airplane slowly climbed through the hot, humid August air, and with the report to Tuscaloosa Tower completed, Rick asked me to begin a slow turn to the right. Here's something I learned in the cockpit: While I may be holding the controls there will be times when in no way do I feel that I am in control. There were just too many things vying for my attention. Even a small single engine airplane has a full complement of panel instruments to be aware of. There is the air speed indicator, the vertical speed indicator, the altimeter, the attitude indicator, the turn coordinator, the inclinometer, the directional gyro and, of course, the RPM indicator. Then there are the many non-flight instruments that are still very important such as oil pressure, alternator, fuel gauges, fuel pressure gauge,

COCKPIT LESSON

While I may be holding the controls there will be times when in no way do I feel that I am in control.

temperature gauge, timer, VOR heads and omni bearing selectors for each. Suspended from the windshield (called a wind screen in aviation) is a floating compass; it indicates the direction of flight but responds to flight input backwards. (you have to turn the airplane to the left to move the compass to the right.) It was like drinking from a fire hose as I tried to be aware of all the information these instruments were providing for me.

As I prepared to begin my first turn in the airplane, I asked Rick, "If I do something wrong, are you able to save us before we hit the ground?" No matter how long I live I will never forget Rick's answer. "I could save us ten times before we hit the ground." When I heard the confidence in him, it built confidence in me. If God could get me to understand how many times He could save me from disaster, perhaps I would trust Him faster.

He had the same issues with the men He surrounded Himself with here on Earth during His three-and-a-half years of ministry. Much like us, they were a little hard of hearing. There's a story in Mark 6:24: "Then He said to them, 'Take heed what you hear. With the same measure you use, it will be measured to you; and to you who hear, more will be given.' " *NKJV* (More on this in Chapter 10)

It is possible to hear the words but not get the message. Jesus would, on the same day, give them a chance to increase their faith through their hearing. I have discovered this:

10

---

*Little faith is always
accompanied by great fear.*

Continuing in the same chapter of Mark, in verse 35 we read, "On the same day, when evening had come, He said to them, 'Let us cross over to the other side.' 36 Now when they had left the multitude, they took Him along in the boat as He was. And other little boats were also with Him. 37 And a great windstorm arose, and the waves beat into the boat, so that it was already filling. 38 But He was in the stern, asleep on a pillow. And they awoke Him and said to Him, "Teacher, do You not care that we are perishing?" 39 Then He arose and rebuked the wind, and said to the sea, "Peace, be still!" And the wind ceased and there was a great calm. 40 But He said to them, "Why are you so fearful? How is it that you have no faith?" 41 And they feared exceedingly, and said to one another, "Who can this be, that even the wind and the sea obey Him!" *NKJV*

They missed it. They heard a word that would have given them faith but they didn't hear the message. The message was, "No matter how bad the wind is blowing, we are going to the other side." He never proposes anything that He doesn't purpose you to succeed in. He didn't promise there would be no resistance, only that there would be no defeat. Be careful how you hear: For to those who hear, more will be given. The absence of faith always produces the idea that God doesn't care about us. "Don't you care that we perish?" they asked Him. What a question to ask the one who had made the lonely trip from Heaven to Earth all because He cared so much.

Pam has said many things that I didn't hear, sometimes because I wasn't listening and sometimes because I wasn't hearing. It is possible to be out of hearing range and it is also possible to be out of interest range. You can be in the same room with someone and still not hear what they're saying to you.

Sight Picture

Now, with confidence that I wasn't going to turn us over and get us into something Rick couldn't get us out of, I approached my first turn. Rick said, "I want you to take a mental sight picture of what you see through the windshield. That is your sight picture of straight and level. We will do the same once we're established in the turn. Making a mental note of what straight and level looked like, I gently leaned the airplane into a shallow bank and pressed the corresponding rudder pedal, which my feet were resting on. Rick had explained to me that by using the pedals to control the rudder and the controls to move the ailerons, we would make a coordinated turn. Once we were established in the turn he said, "Now take a mental sight picture. This is what you're looking for in a 30-degree bank."

As I pondered those lessons I considered the number of times during my flying life I've had to find my way back to straight and level. It is so important that you know what it looks and feels like. How about you? Have you had times when you needed to get back to straight and level in your personal or spiritual life? Perhaps you needed someone to remind you what it looks like because you were so far from it. If you will commit it to memory before you begin the twists and turns, it will be much easier to recognize when it's once again in your windshield.

Unlike driving a car, flying an airplane exposes you to three axes of movement. It's somewhat disconcerting at first, but that's why they call it "flight training." We have to train our brains to think differently. In a car we don't have to deal with the third axis of movement. Our car moves back and forth along a straight line or it turns left or right. Even though a car goes up and down hills, it isn't a third axis of movement because it is running on the rail of Earth's gravity. Suppose somewhere in the process you lose contact with the Earth. If and when that moment comes, a car then experiences three axes of movement because it's no longer tied to the rail of gravity firmly holding it in place. That's what happens in an airplane. It's what birds and flying insects live with every day. No longer can you take it for granted that you will stay straight and level. You actually have to provide input into the airplane controls in order to remain straight and level. If you don't provide that input, gravity will take over and pull you down to the ground, where you will find that you are once again in a two-axes-of-movement paradigm.

So what is the point in this discussion? To highlight the concept that we are not just two-axes-of-movement creations. We are spirit, soul, and body. Your spirit is the part of you that is born again. Your soul (your mind, will and emotions) has to be renewed daily. Your body is the place where these other two live. Understanding this paradigm is imperative to making a safe flight to what's waiting next in your life. We must focus not just on training the mind—as some have done—and ignore the spirit. Nor should we ignore the other two and just train the body. We need all three to live in harmony and balance in order to enjoy a straight and level flight. Because of the existence of gravity, when you begin a turn in an airplane, you have to plan for gravity making an impact on your altitude. Therefore, as we begin a turn, a small amount of backwards pressure on the controls pulls the nose of the airplane up and restores any tendency of altitude loss as the airplane turns. Likewise, as we make turns and changes in our lives, we should lift our head to prevent loss of altitude. What did David write? "But You, O Lord, are a shield for me, My glory and the One who lifts up my head." Psalms 3:3 *NKJV* He also said, "I will lift up my eyes to the hills…" Psalms 121:1a *NKJV*

That first hour of flight training had me hooked. I was more certain than ever that flying was something I wanted to do. Even though I didn't understand it all, and although I had some reservations about doing all this alone, I knew I had discovered a new passion. We made many of those gentle 30 degree turns to the left and the right. Rick made sure that I had regained my confidence before asking me to return to the airport. He made me feel as though I was the best student he'd ever taught. He was the kind of teacher every student needs in order to gain confidence in their ability to accomplish the challenges ahead.

The Big Picture

While the sight picture described in the previous section is important for visually recognizing the aircraft's position, the big picture described here is important for each of us, because if we lose sight of the big picture, we will lose sight of the purpose and plan for the trip. We have to believe that God has a purpose for our life.

A puzzle is just a big picture that's been cut into hundreds of tiny ones.

If you try to put the puzzle together without having a picture of what it's supposed to look like, it is very difficult to complete the project. On the other hand, with the big picture set before you, you can connect the small pieces to each other until they form the larger one.

Before the days of moving maps and in-cockpit weather, it was necessary for me to plan my entire route on what was called sectional charts. These were maps of a section of the United States and they showed the topography located along the way as well as airports, waterways, towers, major highways, and navigational aids with radio frequencies. They would provide the "big picture" and allowed me to prepare myself for the flight. I was first made aware of these charts (maps) very early in my training because there are the bible that pilots live by. They give us the Big Picture of our journey and point out the obvious hazards. What they did not show were the current weather conditions, or other air traffic. That was up to me to discern before and during each flight.

Being aware of what is going on around us is called situational awareness. (I've dedicated an entire chapter to this subject in Chapter 10.) It has cost many pilots and passengers their lives simply because someone wasn't paying attention to their surroundings. Learning to fly taught me so much about this concept. The difference between life and death can be something as subtle as water in the gas that the pilot didn't check, or believing a gas gauge instead of visually checking the gas level. Two things pilots are taught to never believe: 1) A gas gauge, 2) An oil gauge. Always make a visual inspection of both.

If we understand the big picture it makes the small picture easier to process. On occasion I've tried to compare my small picture and small understanding with my lifetime journey. If I understand God's big picture for my life, I stop wrestling with the small steps I take along the way. I made the flight from Tuscaloosa, AL to Saltillo, MX many times. There was no need to start planning my arrival at Laredo until I had crossed the Mississippi River and the marshy swampland of southern Louisiana, and until I had seen the vast open plains of West Texas.

By plotting a course on my charts I knew what to avoid and where I would make planned fuel stops. They gave me the necessary frequencies I'd need in order to communicate along the way. How about our spiritual journey? We all have a course that's been plotted for us and it's up to us to gain access to His plans for our life. If we see His "Big Picture" for our life, we are able to push through some of the places where it might be tempting to quit or it might be easy to stop and build a house where a tent should go.

In the early days of my flying to Mexico and back, I would spend hours poring over my charts and talking to Flight Service. At that time they were an agency within the FAA that provided flight information to pilots. I knew the best airports to stop at for fuel and the ones to avoid. Flight preparation is the best way to have a safe and enjoyable flight. But I'm getting ahead of myself. Let me get back to the big picture. If you want to live at peace with God and understand His plan and purpose for your life, get the big picture firmly imprinted in your heart, and when the discouraging stuff happens, you can say, "Well, no big deal. I know where I'm headed, this must just be a step along the journey."

I will speak more on the subject of situational awareness in a later chapter, (Chapter 10) but for now let me close this chapter with this thought: My tendencies lean more toward "situational unawareness." I could miss seeing a muddy elephant in a snow bank because I'm typically focused on the task at hand. I therefore I need all the help I can get keeping my focus. If you know you have the same tendency as me, the ability to lose sight of the main thing, I suggest finding a way to make yourself see the big picture and keep it in sight. It will make joining the small puzzle pieces together into the finished project easier, making them more suitable for displaying somewhere. That's why I use a check list in the airplane, and a "to-do" list in the office.

CHAPTER 2

STALLS

After that first introductory flight, I was hooked and Rick knew it. My flight training corresponded perfectly with his transition from the Walmart flight department to NetJets, the world's largest private airline. NetJets is the airline of the rich and famous. It was the fall of 2002 and this transition period gave Rick a lot unexpected available time. This time translated into flight training for me. I flew with him every opportunity I got, which was several times a week for the first month.

I was learning the basics of maneuvering the airplane. Take-offs in calm winds were easy to master but landing the airplane was not something he rushed to teach me. Before teaching me to land, he had to teach me about stalls. Landings are the most important and dangerous part of any flight. By their proximity to the ground and your slow airspeed, the danger of an unintentional stall is heightened. Remember, there is a purpose and a process for everything God does in our lives. He doesn't teach us landings until He's taught us stalls.

Stalls are practiced at a safe altitude where flight recovery is easily accomplished. Simply put,

---

A stall is when the airplane stops
flying and starts falling.

Technically put, a stall is what happens when the wing of the airplane stops providing enough lift and it actually quits flying. Remember this: What the Wright brothers discovered wasn't flight, but rather the reason for flight, which is lift.

Flight is accomplished because the air passing over the wing is moving fast enough to produce lift. Have you ever been under a porch or pavilion and noticed the wind was blowing harder and faster under it, than outside of it? The knowledge of this phenomenon is based upon the work of a Swiss mathematician and physicist named Daniel Bernoulli, who lived in the 1700's. He realized that when water or air is constricted, it picks up speed. An example of this is wind blowing through an opening or a river flowing through a canyon. As the canyon walls narrow, space is constricted, and the water speeds up. This is what's happening to the wind blowing under the pavilion. The roof and ground act just like the walls of a canyon, constricting the airflow (instead of water) and as the wind passes through, it speeds up. This is known as Bernoulli's principle.

The same thing happens as wind passes over the wing of an airplane. The wing is typically curved on top, but flat on the bottom. As the wind passes under the wing, it remains at a constant speed, but where the leading edge of the wing divides the wind, it actually speeds up as it passes over the top. As that wind speeds up, it creates an area of low pressure above the wing, which creates lift. Thus, an airplane wing lifts from above not from below. In the same way, your spiritual lift is also coming from above. It is caused by the moving of God's spirit through your life as He gives you wings to soar like an eagle. Perhaps that's why the prophet could write in Isaiah 40:31, "But those who wait on the Lord shall renew their strength; They shall mount up with wings like eagles, They shall run and not be weary, They shall walk and not faint." *NKJV*

Stalls were a part of almost every flight after the first one. I suppose Rick didn't want to scare me on that first flight, but after that, all bets were off. He maintained that teaching stalls early was the key to a long and successful life of flying.

We didn't learn stalls in order
to do them, we learned stalls in order
to recognize and avoid them.

I learned that stalls can only occur when a wing reaches what's known as "critical angle of attack," where the angle of the

21

wing is no longer creating lift. Stalls can occur at any speed if the angle of the wing exceeds its ability to lift. In our life we must also recognize the angle of attack. The devil has one mission in your life: He wants to destroy you. If he can get you off focus and distracted long enough from the sight picture in your windscreen, he will cause you to forget what straight and level flight or coordinated turns look like. He wants to get you so far out of position that your wings stop lifting. There's good news, though: In the event that you get into a stall, it is recoverable as long as your altitude is high enough to allow you time to do so. This is why we practiced stalls at high altitudes, and the reason that landings were not learned until stalls were mastered.

Stalls don't just happen with no warning. There are many warning signs of an impending stall. There are three distinct warnings before every stall, you will see it, hear it, and feel it before a stall occurs. First, an airplane is equipped with an airspeed indicator (speedometer). It has a series of green and white arcs on it which indicate the speed at which a stall will occur. The green arc represents the airspeed in a clean configuration, meaning no flaps extended. The white arc represents the speed at which the stall occurs, with flaps extended. Second, every airplane is equipped with what's called a stall horn. This is a wind-activated switch, mounted on the leading edge of the wing. This switch will only be activated when the angle of attack reaches the point that wind pushes the switch upwards. The stall horn sounds at five knots (speed) faster than a stall. So, when the stall horn sounds you know that a stall is imminent if you don't correct something soon. How would you like to have one of those for your life? Well you do. It's called your conscience. As long as you listen to it and don't ignore it, your Holy Spirit-activated conscience will sound an alarm when you are nearing the threat of a stall. The problem occurs when we don't listen to it.

If a pilot ignores the stall horn, the last and final sign before a stall occurs is more drastic. The airplane actually begins to buffet. You will feel the whole airplane begin to shake as the wings stop providing lift. This buffeting is the last warning you're going to receive before the nose of the airplane literally drops toward the Earth. Here is where Rick taught me the first and greatest commandment of flight, which I have never forgotten, nor do I intend to.

"Maintain thy airspeed lest the ground
rise up and smite thee." ~Rick Price

I have flown by that rule since August 2002 and have never unintentionally stalled an airplane. Here's something I've learned in the cockpit: If I stay on top of my spiritual life, keep my airspeed up, and my angle of attack within tolerances, I will never stall.

So how do we recover from a stall? That's a great question, since we have to get the airplane flying again or the consequences will be devastating. Recovery is easy: Push forward on the yoke (controls) to lower the nose of the airplane, add power, (full throttle), watch the airspeed indicator climb and then slowly pull back on the yoke until straight and level flight

COCKPIT LESSON

If I stay on top of my spiritual life, keep my airspeed up, and my angle of attack within tolerances, I will never stall.

is achieved. There may be times when you feel you're stalling in your spiritual flight as well. If so, lower your nose (humble yourself), add power (Jesus said, "You shall receive power…," Acts 1:8), pick up speed and gently lift your head to a straight and level flight.

During my first few stalls, which were demonstrated for me, I think I held my breath but was completely confident in Rick's ability to maneuver the airplane. Still, they scared me. Rick said that was a good thing, it would help me keep my airspeed up during landings. The white and green arcs on an airspeed indicator show the speeds at which stalls will occur. There are several types of stalls:

- Power on stalls: Stalls that occur during powered flight.

- Power off stalls: Stalls that occur during reduced or low power settings.

- Fully configured: Flaps extended to provide more lift.

- Clean: No flaps extended.

- Turning stalls: Stalls that occur during a turn (could possibly happen in a traffic pattern).

- Straight ahead stalls: Stalls that occur during straight flight (such as landing).

Watching your airspeed indicator and its corresponding color-coded arc will keep you from making the drastic mistake of a stall close to the ground during a landing. Mistakes of this kind are usually fatal. There is no time for recovery from a stall during take-off and landing. Likewise, we must remind ourselves of the eternal consequence of our actions and lifestyles. We are not promised tomorrow, only that He who holds it will somehow guide us on and off the runway.

During my training, I was required to maintain slow flight and keep the stall horn sounding while gently turning left and right. (This was all done at 2000 feet MSL or higher) Once again, this is done to teach us that the stall horn means "impending stall," not "stall." You can actually fly an airplane while keeping the stall horn blasting and never actually stall. I've seen some Christian believers who insisted upon living their life in this manner. They were more concerned about, "What can I get away with?" than "What can I get away from?" It's better to live your life trying to see how close to Jesus you can get, rather than how close to the world you can live. It wasn't until I had learned to maneuver the airplane just above a stall, that Rick allowed me to land for the first time.

From the very first flight, I had been required to hold the yoke, while Rick actually did the landing. This was done in order to allow me to feel the process. I was not allowed to maneuver the controls on my own, however, only to follow the movement and input that he made. Gradually, the responsibly shifted. Rick inputted less and less, and I inputted more and more until finally, I made my first successful landing. I remember; that first landing was a little like getting shot down, but with Rick's help I learned how to slow the airplane to just above a stall, and then set it down on the center line of the runway just as the stall horn sounded. That's what's described as the perfect landing. The stall horn should be sounding as the wheels make contact with the runway. Getting everything synchronized is the challenge.

No matter how well you plot your course, navigate your flight, avoid turbulence, and communicate with air traffic control, your passengers will largely base their opinion of your skills as a pilot upon how well you land the plane. If everything else goes perfectly but you bounce down the runway like a dolphin in the wake of a ship, your passengers will leave the airport saying, "I'm not getting back in a plane with him until he learns to fly."

Likewise, it is the landing at your destiny and calling that is so important to you. Arriving at an airport is only part of the flight. Getting safely on the ground is the most important part. Many people have been killed trying to land at their destination airport, and all because they didn't pay attention to the warning signs of a stall. If you break the first and greatest commandment of flight and fail to maintain your airspeed during the final approach to landing, you will stall too close to the ground to recover. There are three distinct warnings before a stall: You will see it, hear it, and feel it before it occurs. Heed the warnings and you will survive; ignore them, and it will be your last mistake.

Spins

Spins are extremely dangerous and to an unsuspecting pilot, often fatal. Spins can only occur when an airplane experiences an uncoordinated stall, meaning the yaw (left and right of the tail of the airplane) is skewed to one side or the other. As the airplane stalls uncoordinated, the uncoordinated wing drops first causing the airplane to enter a spin.

Private pilot training includes practicing recovery from stalls. However, it does not currently include spin training because of the danger of unnecessarily exposing young pilots to them. Instead, instructors focus on eliminating stalls and thus eliminating spins. If you never stall, you will never spin. Even a stunt pilot performing spins at an airshow has to stall the airplane in order to enter a spin.

As you may or may not know, the flight controls in an airplane are really quite simple. You pull back on the yoke to go up, and push forward on the yoke to go down.

As airspeed slows we pull back on the yoke to continue maintaining the altitude we are flying at. The slower the airspeed, the more angle is required to fly at the same altitude. As the angle changes, the coefficient of lift along the wing also changes, moving us closer and closer to a stall and a potential spin. A stall always precedes the spin but only by a few seconds. It's not just a stall, it's an uncoordinated stall that produces the spin. We can stall the airplane a hundred times and never enter a spin. Stalling is dangerous but an uncoordinated stall is vicious. The reason it is so dangerous is because to get out of a spin, the pilot must do the opposite of what got him into it to begin with.

In Luke 10 there is a story about two sisters, one named Martha and one named Mary. Their brother was the Lazarus that Jesus raised from the dead. In the story in Luke, Jesus has come to their house and Martha is busy preparing a meal for Jesus when she becomes angry that her sister is not helping to serve.

Martha was moving closer and closer towards a stall as she was busily trying to do something for Jesus that He had not even asked for. Do you ever do that? The stall is bad enough, but if it's uncoordinated, she will enter a spin, and while recovery is possible, unless correctly briefed and executed, it could end tragically.

Five steps to spin recovery (remember, this is done while you're looking straight down at the ground spinning in the windscreen and adrenaline coursing through your system):

1. Power off: Pull the power setting to idle to arrest the fall.

2. Full and opposite rudder: Fully depress the rudder pedal which is opposite to the direction the plane is turning. (i.e., If the plane is spinning to the right, push the left pedal, etc.)

3. Full forward on controls: Push the controls to the full forward position, even though your mind is telling you "forward on the controls makes you go down." Do it anyway, you're already falling, how could it get any worse?

4. As the spin stops, slowly pull back on the controls and allow the airplane to regain altitude back to level flight.

5. Apply power to maintain straight and level flight.

The natural tendency of a pilot is to pull back on the yoke first in order to arrest the spin. After all, we're taught from early on that's what makes the airplane climb, and it does any other time. However, pulling back on the yoke during a spin only intensifies the spin and causes the airplane to corkscrew downward even tighter. It's called a death spiral.

To better understand the reason behind the instructions, just look at the tail of an airplane. During a spin the rudder, which is the vertical fin on the tail is turned at nearly 90° angle making it function like the elevator, and the elevator, which is the horizontal part of the tail, is acting as the rudder.

Only full and opposite depression of the rudder and full forward on the yoke will recover the plane from a spin. These actions may seem illogical at the time, but in reality they are the only thing that will cause recovery. Here's something I've learned in the cockpit: When my life is in a spin, it's only by doing the opposite of what put me into the spin that will deliver me. If I've stopped reading my bible, I must start again. If I've stopped praying, I must start again. If I've started complaining and focusing on the negative, I have to realign my mouth with the word of God. Only changing what put me into the spin in the first place is going to get me out of it.

COCKPIT LESSON

When my life is in a spin, it's only by doing the opposite of what put me into the spin that will deliver me.

If your life is in a spin today, you must change what you're doing and stop the spin, then you can pull out of the plunge.

CHAPTER 3

SOLO FLIGHT

F uel, mixture, carb-heat. Fuel, mixture, carb-heat. Fuel, mixture, carb-heat. I was so used to hearing those words I said them in my sleep. This was the mantra I recited during every approach to landing. There are various rhythmic sayings throughout flight training that instructors will give their students to help them poetically remember the process, but this was the one Rick had taught me since the very first flight. For non-fliers let me interpret:

- **Fuel:** It refers to confirming the position of the fuel selector. The Cessna 172 has LEFT, RIGHT and BOTH: It should be on the BOTH setting.

- **Mixture:** This refers to the gas/air mixture knob controlled by the pilot.

- **Carb-heat:** This is the carburetor heat knob used to prevent icing in the carburetor. When pulled, it diverts warm air from the engine to surround the carburetor.

I was about 15 hours into my training when Rick began telling me that I was nearing the time to solo. Remember my fear from Chapter One? "There's no way I could ever do this alone." Suddenly that thing which I had pushed to the back of my mind came rushing to the forefront again. What's he talking about? Is he sure I can do this? Does he think I'm ready for this? What if I forget something important? These and a dozen more questions were pounding in my head but I listened to my instructor's calm voice and soon realized, "He has more confidence in me than I have in myself." Here's something I've learned in the cockpit: "Based upon the assignments Jesus has given me, I often feel that He has more confidence in me than I have in myself as well".

By this time I was comfortable with climbs, turns, descents, landings and even stalls (to the point that knew I could avoid one). I had been required to begin radio communication early on and was comfortable talking to Tuscaloosa Tower. By the time I had 15 hours of training, Rick began giving me what I call "The silent treatment." He sat quietly in the copilot seat while I preformed all the procedures I would need to accomplish my first solo. Have you ever felt like God was giving you the silent

COCKPIT LESSON

"Based upon the assignments Jesus has given me, I often feel that He has more confidence in me than I have in myself as well".

treatment? You know He's onboard yet He's not saying anything? It's like He's waiting until you make a mistake and then suddenly swoops in and rescues you.

You're thankful for His presence
but you long for His voice.

Did I make that turn right? Was I too slow on my approach? Did I lose the right amount of altitude on base leg? Did I engage my flaps too soon? Was my landing smooth?

In a way, it was more nerve racking with Rick sitting quietly doing nothing, than the actual solo. The other side of that coin, however, was that with him in the airplane, I knew if I did something wrong he would come to my rescue. During the actual solo, I knew I had to get it right. A beautiful fact about all trainer airplanes is that they are very forgiving. Perfection is pursued but not required. There is a large envelope of tolerance in the way a Cessna 172 flies and even though there are some unbreakable laws that must be followed, these airplanes almost fly themselves if we give them the chance. This is the same way it is with God, we may strive for perfection, but the knowledge that our weakness is made perfect by His strength lifts us ever higher in our pursuit of Him until literally, *the sky is the limit* to what we can experience on our journey to knowing Him. He is filled with grace for those who try.

There are some absolutes which we cannot compromise, but His love and tolerance are far greater than we understand.

I shall never forget the day of my solo flight. It was October 24, 2002 at Tuscaloosa, AL (KTCL) at 4:30 in the afternoon. A solo flight is designed and planned to be simple, short and uneventful. To complete the qualification, a student must perform three takeoffs and landings to a full stop. He must taxi back to the departure end of the runway for each takeoff. This gives the student time to confirm that the airplane is in a clean configuration for the next takeoff. Under normal takeoff conditions the flaps are retracted, fuel is set to full mixture (at airports that are not at high elevations) and carb heat is off. Changing some or all of these components can greatly impact the takeoff roll and put the student in danger.

Tuscaloosa is a controlled airport (i.e., there is a control tower on the field). I can remember Rick saying to me, "You're ready. Let me out." I think I swallowed my gum as I looked at him with questions on my face. His reassuring voice convinced me that I could do it. When the passenger door closed and I was all alone in that little cockpit for the first time, I felt the cool wind from the propeller blowing through the window and the steady hum of the engine. Suddenly I was confident I could do it. That fear of doing this alone, which I described in Chapter One, was gone. I knew that my instructor had confidence in me and had seen a demonstration of my ability through the hours of training he'd given me. This was the moment I had dreaded and dreamed of. I know that seems like a conflict in terms, yet have you ever wanted to do something so badly but when the time came you weren't sure you could go through with it? It's in moments like that when you must trust the instructor, push the throttle to the firewall, and start the plane moving. It's the sitting still that torments you. Once the plane starts moving and you're committed to the takeoff roll, you're forced to do what you've been trained for: Fly!

Asking for and receiving my clearance to taxi from the ramp to the hold line of runway 22, I told myself, "There's no real danger, you're just taxiing now, there's still time to back out." As I taxied up to the hold line of the runway and set the break, I began methodically going through my pre-takeoff check list. I did not skip any part of it, just as I do not omit anything today after more than 2000 hours of flight time. There are just some things that are indispensable and a pre-flight checklist is one of them. First I confirmed that all gauges in the panel were indicating the correct values. I checked all of the control surfaces (flaps, rudder, and elevator) and confirmed what I already knew to be true: That everything was moving unrestricted. I did an engine run-up and checked both magnetos to confirm spark. I pulled the carburetor heat on and confirmed RPM drop, which indicated that it was operational. I checked the alternator and electrical system. I confirmed the fuel selector valve was set to both tanks. Suddenly, like a monster staring me in the face, I realized I was at the end of the check list and all confirmations were complete. It was time to fly or go home. Has that time ever come for you? Maybe an opportunity to fulfill a desire or dream has been given to you but fear kept you from moving forward. There was only one thing in that cockpit standing between me and my dream of flying: Me.

Pushing through my hesitation I told myself, "You're ready. You're equal to the task." I switched the radio frequency to 121.30 and said, "Tuscaloosa Tower, N6545D is at the hold line of runway 22 ready to go. I'll be staying in the pattern." The tower operator, knowing I was a student pilot, spoke slowly and clearly for my benefit, "N6545D cleared for takeoff runway 22, make left closed traffic." This meant I was to stay in the traffic pattern (see glossary of terms) and make left turns.

*Fear is not something to be afraid of,
but something to be used like a tool.*

It sharpens our performance, just as a whetstone sharpens the blade of a knife. Preparation had brought me to the point of opportunity and now I was ready for the first solo flight of my life.

I advanced the throttle just enough to start the plane moving and to roll into position. For all of us, getting into position for a takeoff is the key. As I crossed the hold line I knew that takeoff was imminent. I pointed the nose of that little airplane down runway 22 and paused just long enough to say a short prayer. "Lord keep me safe."

I wiped the sweat from the palms of my hands, pushed the throttle all the way to the firewall and the plane began to roll forward. Just as if Rick was sitting in the seat beside me, I kept my focus on the runway ahead and the airspeed indicator on the panel. I rehearsed the first and greatest commandment Rick had taught me,

---

"Maintain thy airspeed lest the
ground rise up and smite thee."

As the speed climbed to 30, 40, 50, then 55 knots, so did my excitement. I was committed and there was no stopping me. Between 55 and 60 knots I gently pulled back on the controls. As the wheels of that Cessna 172 left contact with the runway and stopped spinning, the nose of that little airplane began climbing heavenward, just as my spirits were also doing.

It was as if time stood still. Have you ever pursued something for a long time and then finally caught it? You wanted to savor the moment but knew that if you did you would miss the next thing that was happening? I set my climb speed at 65 knots and watched the airspeed indicator like a cat watches a mouse hole. I could hear Rick's voice in my head, and continued maintaining my airspeed. There was no way I was falling below 65 knots on my climb. From the hours spent working on practice maneuvers I knew that the airplane was engineered to fly if the pilot kept it between the correct parameters. I was determined to do that. As I reached 900 feet MSL I knew it was time to turn the crosswind leg (see glossary of terms). Gone was the fear of turning that had once plagued me. I now knew that the airplane would continue flying, even though I was turning. There will come times in your life when fear will be speaking in one ear and faith in the other.

*The key to overcoming what fear
is saying is to make your faith speak louder
than your fear.*

Sitting adjacent to the airport in Tuscaloosa is a Goodyear tire plant. When departing runway 22 and remaining in a left traffic pattern, your flight path takes you directly over the factory. Depending upon the winds aloft and the activity below, there is frequently a little turbulence as you cross the plant. I suppose it's from the heat rising from the tire manufacturing process. As I turned downwind and felt the jostling of the 172 crossing the turbulence, I knew I wasn't going to fall out of the sky, but there was that brief moment when fear and faith had a confrontation. Yet, what was I going to do? I was 1000 feet above the ground. I was committed to the fight. There was nothing left to do but continue. There have been times in my life since then, when faced with a challenge or a difficult situation, I have called upon that same blind faith and just kept flying. What options do we really have? Something else I've learned in the cockpit: Keep flying, destiny is on the other side of the turbulence.

As I reached the midway point of the downwind leg, I recited the mantra "Fuel, mixture, carb-heat," and went through the landing checklist. I adjusted the throttle, pushed the fuel mixture to rich, and pulled on the carb-heat. I pushed the flaps switch and an electric motor lowered the flaps to 10 degrees. I was nearing the time for my turn to base leg, which includes a 500 foot decent. I had done this scores of times with Rick and knew exactly when to make that turn and start my decent. Without warning however, and without expecting it, Tuscaloosa Tower called "N6545D extend your downwind for incoming traffic. I'll call your base leg." Wow, something different than I had expected. I hadn't practiced this. There's no way to predict some events which could affect your flight. You see, life doesn't care if you're a first time solo pilot or an experienced ace. It may throw you a curve ball. Things happen, and when they do, it's our training that prepares us or fails us. Without missing a beat I answered the controller, "N6545D extending downwind leg." Of course today a little thing like turbulence or a change in a clearance to landing instructions doesn't even make the concern list, however, on a first solo flight it was challenging.

COCKPIT LESSON

Keep flying, destiny is on the other side of the turbulence.

Finally the call from came Tuscaloosa tower "N6545D thank you for your help, start your base turn, runway 22, cleared for landing." Finally, I was on my way to the runway. But now I was out of position. I was a half mile further downwind than where I had practiced so many times. There is a rule of thumb that says, "Start base leg when the runway numbers are at a 45 degree angle off your shoulder. Lose 500 feet of altitude on base and 500 feet on final approach." This rule works great at uncontrolled airports where you're calling your own turns, but tower operators are under no such obligation. Now, being further downwind when I made my turn to base I had to change my decent rate on final approach. I looked to the left of the runway and saw the four-light VASI (visual approach slope indicator). I remembered what Rick had taught me about the VASI and knew that it would get me safely to the numbers of a runway anytime I could see them. There are two red lights and two white lights on a VASI. I could hear Rick in my head, "White over white, you're high as a kite, Red over red, you'll be dead, red over white and you're just right." I adjusted my decent so that I had two white lights and two red lights and followed them all the way to the runway.

A solo departure is certainly a milestone in any pilot's training, but it's the safe landing, I mean the one that doesn't tear anything up, that really indicates you're learning as a student. When the wheels made contact with the runway for my first solo

THE SKY'S THE LIMIT

landing I was just past the numbers on runway 22. I slowed the airplane to a safe speed and then took the taxiway exit the controller had given me. It was time now to taxi back to the hold line and repeat the process. It had only taken about ten minutes for that first traffic pattern flight, but it felt like an hour had passed. As I taxied back for the second flight, my confidence was high and I felt faith rising to a new level. After preparing the airplane for the next takeoff, I called Tuscaloosa Tower and was once again given my clearance to depart and remain in the pattern. I completed the next two flights without complications and returned to the FBO where Rick and Pam were waiting for me.

To cheers and pats on the back we returned the keys of the airplane to Bama Air. In the lobby Rick did the customary thing of any new solo pilot, he cut the back out of my shirt and wrote the date and pertinent information on it with a black marker. I still have that shirt framed and on the wall of my office. The owner of Bama Air and of N6545D, Danny Dubose, became a lifelong friend of Pam and me and has served on the board of Latin American Ministry since its inception in 2003.

A solo license does not a pilot make, but I was on my way and excited to be able to fly alone legally and to build time in the air. Now with a sign off in my flight log from Rick, I was ready to continue my training, much of which would be alone. In the coming chapters I will share more of those moments, and lessons I learned from the left seat of a small plane. Even if you're not a pilot or aspiring to be one, there are things that you will face in life, which these chapters will help you deal with. Let's continue our journey together and remember, The Sky's The Limit to what you can do and where you can go with God.

CHAPTER 4

SLAYING THE DRAGON

After my solo flight things began moving faster for me. Now that I had a license to fly alone I went to the airport often and worked in the traffic pattern on takeoffs and landings. A deep respect for flying began to develop within me. I longed to learn more and more but still carried a deep uncertainty about both my own ability and that of the airplane. Even though I had, by this time, read mountains of narrative about flying, and I was trying to keep pace on the academic side of the process, I was not at all convinced that I could manage an airplane in windy conditions. Thus, I only flew on non-windy days or on days when the wind corresponded well with the runway directions.

Rick was working for NetJets by this time and was frequently gone for several days at a time. During one of these weeks away he left me with an assignment. "I want you to fly to Greensboro, AL airport, land and return to Tuscaloosa." Now, I know that sounds easy as you read it in this book, but here are the details and the story of that flight.

Greensboro, AL (7A0) is 32 nautical miles almost due south from Tuscaloosa. In those days I was not using a GPS to navigate, even though many airplanes had them, I was not allowed to use one. I was being taught "old school," which meant pilotage and dead reckoning. This was the navigation method used by early pilots and is still very important to pilots today. It enables you to find your destination in the unlikely event of equipment failure. I had taken my sectional chart, plotted the short course and noted highways, rivers, lakes and railroads that would help me find my way. I knew that coming home would be a snap since it would be impossible to miss I-59/20 running east to west across the state, with Tuscaloosa sitting alongside it. Going south, however, I would cross the interstate immediately and proceed into a less-populated area of Alabama. This would not only be a lesson in landing at an uncontrolled airport, but it would also be a short version of the solo-cross country trip I would be required to take before I could take my check ride.

It was a beautiful day that I had chosen for this adventure but not calm winds by any means. Being very eager to complete my assignment, I decided to depart in spite of the wind, figuring I could always just circle the airport and come home. I performed the customary pre-flight inspection, started the engine, requested taxi instruction and prepared to begin the short 20 minute flight. As I rolled down the runway and lifted off into the warm Alabama air, I felt like an airline pilot embarking on a long flight, or a Navy aviator on a secret mission. Reality set in, however, as I leveled off at 2k feet and started looking for recognizable landmarks that would tell me I was on the right track.

As I crossed the interstate and entered the area that Rick and I, and other students, used for a designated practice area, everything was familiar. Soon however, I was leaving familiar ground and looking for highway 69, which I knew would take me to Greensboro. This was the first time I'd flown away from the places I was accustomed to and the first time I would be required to locate and land at an airport that I was unfamiliar with. Rick was confident I could do it and his confidence was contagious. Have you ever noticed how important it is to hang around the right kind of people? Now don't get me wrong, I'm not talking about thinking you're better than anyone.

There is a big difference between prejudice and preference.

If the crowd you're hanging with and spending the majority of your time with isn't inspiring you to become better, you might want to enlarge your circle. If you're the smartest one in your group, your group is too small. If you're the most talented person in the band, get in a different band. Being the most gifted and smartest person in your circle will never produce a better you. I would rather be around people who pull me up than those who pull me down.

Everything looks different from the air. Our three-dimensional world becomes one dimensional as you look down from an airplane. Greensboro, AL is just a dot on the map. It's just a wide spot on highway 69. The airport almost takes up more real estate than the town. I had flown about 20 minutes when I began to see what looked to me like a runway. It had been easy to find and Rick had known all along that if I would just follow a 180° heading, I would see the town and the airport is just west of there. It was a lesson I would use over and over again in my flying journeys. Part of plotting any course is to place the E6B on a sectional chart and turn the compass to determine the heading. Here's another lesson from the cockpit for you: Once you know the heading you need to fly, if you continue on that heading, you will eventually arrive at your destination, regardless of how long it takes. (A lesson I would need traveling back and forth to Mexico in the coming years.) Now it is much easier to get a heading when planning a flight. Computers and GPS's changed everything but if needed, every pilot must know how to do it the old fashion way.

COCKPIT LESSON

Once you know the heading you need to fly, if you continue on that heading, you will eventually arrive at your destination, regardless of how long it takes.

A long line of pine trees sat adjacent to the runway and I was excited when I had located it. I entered the traffic pattern and began preparing the airplane for landing. Just as I had done dozens of times at Tuscaloosa, I went through the same midfield mantra, "Fuel, mixture, carb-heat." I set my flaps to the customary 10 degrees for downwind, called my base-leg and began a 500 foot decent while also increasing my flaps to 20 degrees. Soon I could feel the surface winds pushing on the airplane. I was nervous but decided to continue the process; I turned final approach and increased to full flaps. With the runway now looming in front of me, I could feel the winds pushing me to the right. What had been a headwind departing Tuscaloosa was now a cross wind as I lined up for landing on runway 36 (The runway numbers represent the runway alignment with a compass with one number missing. In this case, runway 36 is a cardinal heading of 360 degrees.) As I descended, the ride got rougher and harder to control. To best understand how turbulence is generated, think about a rocky stream. The rapids created in a river as the water flows over the rocks, are the same thing that's happening with the air as it flows over trees, buildings, and hills on the ground.

Remember that long row of pine trees I mentioned adjacent to the runway? Well, that row of trees was doing the same thing to my landing as rocks do to your boat in rapids. I was bouncing and jerking around like a tiny boat in a river. I didn't know then what I know now about landing in crosswinds. I didn't understand that I have control over my airplane, even though I have no control over my environment. My situation may be windy and rough, but the ailerons and rudder on an airplane will provide situational stability even in the midst of instability, provided I know how to use them. Remembering what Paul wrote to the Ephesians is so important to safely navigating turbulent times in our lives: "That we should no longer be children, tossed to and fro and carried about with every wind of doctrine, by the trickery of men, in the cunning craftiness of deceitful plotting, but, speaking the truth in love, may grow up in all things into Him who is the head—Christ." Ephesians 4:14-15 *NKJV*.

Well, there I was 500 feet above the ground and descending. I was watching as the numbers 36 got larger and larger in the windscreen. They were growing just as my fear was. It was decision time and I made one at about 250 feet AGL. Trembling from trepidation and remembering there was safety in altitude, I pulled back on the controls, applied full power and climbed out of the turbulence. I felt more relief than shame as the I climbed back to a safe altitude and out of danger. Better to abort a landing than complete a crash, I thought to myself. I knew that the skill needed to land in a high crosswind environment was available to me, but not yet prepared in me. There are times in our lives when we must accept the things we can't change and focus on the things we can. That was one of those times for me.

I completed the short flight back to Tuscaloosa, landed easily with a headwind instead of a crosswind and parked the airplane feeling a bit defeated. That day at Greensboro defeated me but set me on a course and helped me make up my mind on something. I had a decision to make.

Since crosswinds and turbulence are a potential part of every flight, either I would learn to navigate them, or I would stay on the ground.

I called Rick that night and told him what had happened. I probably painted the scene more challenging than it really was, but at any rate I will never forget what Rick told me. His words still ring in my ears today. "When I get home we'll go back to Greensboro together and slay that dragon." Instead of making fun of me or chiding me for my fear, he praised me. "You made the right decision Jim! Good flying starts with good decision making and you made the right one." Choosing your battles while you're learning to fight, builds not only your confidence, but also your competence. With time, giants that loom large today will diminish in size tomorrow. Did you ever notice how much larger things seemed when you were a child? Did you ever return to the place you where you grew up and noticed that nothing is as big as it seemed then? The same thing happens with things you're afraid of and not prepared for. The more practice you put into a thing, the easier it becomes. Some people call it luck. There is an old quote attributed to Arnold Palmer which says, "The more I practice, the luckier I get." The truth is the quote has been around much longer than Arnold Palmer and is attributed to many people. Regardless of who said it, it is nonetheless true.

Practice not only makes perfect, it makes sense. I had faced what appeared to me to be a dragon at the time, but if faced with the same landing components today, it wouldn't even get my attention. We all deal with challenges differently, *how* you do it isn't important, *that* you do it is all that matters.

So within a few days Rick came home from his tour of duty with NetJets and we scheduled a flight back to Greensboro. For me, it was important that it be a day with similar wind conditions, and for my benefit it was. With my instructor seated in the cockpit beside me, my willingness to try was bolstered. It was on this flight I learned another powerful lesson in the cockpit: While I can't control my circumstances, I can control my response.

COCKPIT LESSON

While I can't control my circumstances, I can control my response.

An airplane is equipped with six moving surfaces: Two flaps, two ailerons, one elevator and one rudder. These movable surfaces are controlled by the pilot and are used to positionally align the airplane on a three-axis-of-movement course. As the airplane approaches the runway it acts as a wind vane and naturally points in the direction of the prevailing wind. So while the runway may be oriented at 360 degrees, (Runway 36) the wind may be blowing at 330 degrees causing the nose of the airplane to point that way. Well, you can't land with the nose pointed at a 30 degree angle to the runway. So how do we get the airplane pointed down the runway and keep the wind from shoving us off course? Here's the process. On final approach, as you descend from 500 feet AGL, allow the wind vane effect to occur. It feels weird but don't be alarmed, we don't fly feelings, (That's called flying by the seat of your pants.) We fly by established laws that work every time regardless of feelings. Next, at about treetop height above the runway, use the rudder to straighten the lateral alignment of the airplane so that it's pointing straight down the runway, simultaneously raise the aileron on the windward side of the plane, while this action will lower the wing slightly, it will also keep the airplane from being blown off course.

Rather than actually landing on that first approach, Rick flew the length of the runway keeping us right on the center line and demonstrating the airplane's ability to hold its position and defy the wind's ability to blow us off course. It was amazing and eye opening to me.

After that experience I would go to the airport on windy days just to practice my cross wind landings. I have safely landed in windy conditions that would keep others from flying. I have flown in the challenging West Texas winds and the plains of South Dakota and Wyoming. I have landed in the mountains of Mexico and at some the busiest airports in the south because Rick took the time to properly teach me how to navigate windy conditions.

51

I made the decision that day that I would not let the wind keep me on the ground.

Even though the wind may be blowing in your life, every believer has a power inside of them that will keep them from being blown off course. He is the anchor of your soul. He is the strong tower you can run to, a solid rock and a mighty fortress.

Fear not! Let the wind blow. Jesus will slay the dragon that's roaring at you.

CHAPTER 5

SOLO CROSS COUNTRY

Every pilot, before they can take their check ride with a Federal Aviation Administration examiner, must complete a solo cross country flight. I won't bore you with all the legal requirements but here are some of the basic rules of that flight:

A student pilot:

- Must have the endorsement of a certified flight instructor to complete the flight.

- Must use aeronautical charts for VFR navigation using pilotage and dead reckoning with the aid of a magnetic compass.

- The solo cross-country flight must be at least 150 nautical miles (280 km) total distance, with full-stop landings at a minimum of three points and with one segment of the flight consisting of a straight-line distance of at least 50 nautical miles (93 km) between the takeoff and landing locations.

After months of dual instruction with Rick Price and hours of solo flying locally, the day finally arrived for my solo cross country. I had planned and prepared for the event. It was my birthday, December 16, 2002.

My route complied with all the distance requirements as well as getting to have lunch with my parents who live near Camden, TN. The route was:

KTCL - KMSL - Tuscaloosa, AL - Muscle Shoals, AL

KMSL - 0M4 - Muscle Shoals, AL - Camden, TN

0M4 - 0M1 - Camden, TN - Parsons, TN (Scott field is now gone)

0M1 - KTCL - Parsons, TN - Tuscaloosa, AL

(See figure 5a of proposed route, excluding Parsons, TN)

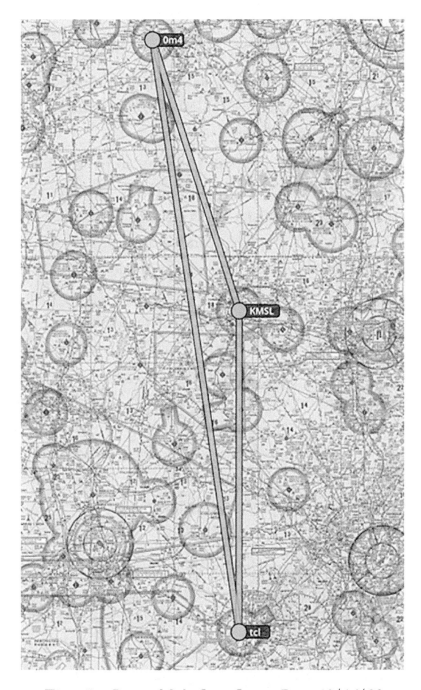

Figure 5a - Proposed Solo Cross-Country Route 12/16/02

I had a total of 340 nautical miles in my proposed solo cross country, more than double the required 150 miles. Upon completing my flight training and getting my license, I was planning to fly back and forth to Mexico, so I started planning long flights from the very beginning.

I remember taking out the sectional maps which would cover my proposed flight, marking a straight line between the waypoints and highlighting it with a marker for easy reference in the cockpit. The U.S. is broken up into sections and each sectional contains all the pertinent information needed for that area. Sectionals are roadmaps for pilots. Each airport is marked on the map along with the elevation, along with runways and other information. Also on the map are major highways, railroads, towers, rivers and lakes, all of which is to keep us from getting lost. There is other information but I will disregard it for the purpose of this book. Suffice it to say that each sectional is a roadmap to get you to the location you're trying to reach. Learning to read it, understand it and then transfer the information from it to the ground we're flying over, is called "pilotage."

If we can understand that a map enables us to find our destinations, why can't we understand that God's word is a map that enables us to find our way to our destinies?

By reading and understanding both, we make our way along the journey from one waypoint to the next. "Your word is a lamp to my feet And a light to my path." Psalm 119:105 *NKJV*

December 16th dawned overcast and windy, but not enough to stop me from making the flight. I had long since conquered that dragon. I had learned my lesson about winds and was not letting it stop the greatest moment of my life. I was about to get in an airplane, by myself, and fly to Tennessee and back. The cloud base was at about 3000 feet along most of the route, but that still left plenty of room for me to fly at 2500 feet and complete my anticipated journey. For all the plans you will make in your life, here is another lesson I learned in the cockpit: "Your flight will largely be determined by the weather on the day of your departure. The operative word is: Flexible." While I would have much preferred to be flying high under a clear sky, I adjusted to the 3000 foot overcast and moved with the new plan. There is no place for complaining, either go or don't go, but don't spend the journey complaining about the conditions.

COCKPIT LESSON

"Your flight will largely be determined by the weather on the day of your departure. The operative word is: Flexible."

Rick and I met for breakfast that morning and went over my flight plan. He approved of both the weather and my proposed route. Together we calculated the winds aloft based upon Flight Service's forecast. As a young pilot you learn how much course correction will be needed to continue to fly a straight line with the wind blowing across your flight path. Here's an example: If the heading to your destination is 360 degrees but the wind is blowing at 30 knots from 270 degrees, you will need to fly a heading of 346 degrees to get to your destination. If you ignore the 14 degree correction needed, and insist on flying the uncorrected heading you will miss your destination completely because the wind will blow you off course. (See Figure 5a)

The same can be said regarding our lives. There are corrections that have to be made in our trajectory or we will miss our destiny. I know that it sounds like a contradiction in terms to discuss missing a destiny. (Since destinies are destiny) However, insisting on your way when God is trying to correct you will result in arriving at some alternate destination and/or perhaps never seeing the plan that God intended for your life. Since we don't know the opposing wind direction or its speed, asking for and receiving course corrections from Him is imperative for us all.

Remember this: "It's not the way your nose is pointed that determines your destination, it's the direction of travel, which determines that."

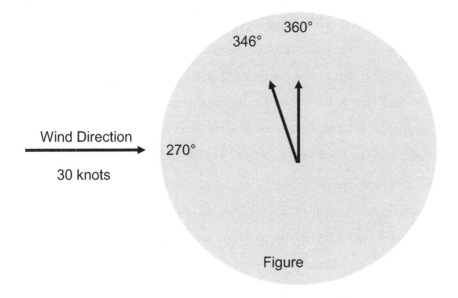

Figure

The Flight

I arrived at the airport, got the keys to N5082G and headed to the Cessna 172 airplane. Were you ever eager but nervous at the same time? I was feeling a little of both, but excitement outweighed any jitters I was feeling. This was my big moment and I was not going to let fear keep me on the ground. I had reached forty-four years old that day, and I was chasing a dream I'd had since I was a teenager. I remember the feeling of achievement I felt as I put my flight bag and headphones in the plane and started my preflight checklist. Even though today I have more than two thousand hours of flight time, a preflight checklist is still a personal requirement for myself. I never depart a runway without first going through a checklist to confirm I've done everything in my power to maintain safety. I know my ability to forget, so I put it in black and white and keep it before my eyes. We have a checklist for our personal lives as well, it's God's word. His word will give you direction. At times it will correct your decisions and even challenge your behavior, but in the end, it will save your soul. I require the same things of myself in my personal walk. I read, quote, and/or meditate on my checklist daily.

During preparation for my solo cross-country Rick had required me to plot, plan and file our trips. One such trip was on 11/26/02 just 20 days before my solo cross-country. Rick had questioned me about the weather and I reported to him that there was an overcast east of the field but that it would probably not impact our flight. My eagerness to fly was stronger than my caution to stay on the ground. I felt that we could get below the cloud base and make the trip successfully. He conceded, and away we went. He was teaching me a valuable lesson which would soon be played out before my eyes and in my windscreen. It would keep me from making a tragic mistake later on as a licensed pilot, but one still not trained to deal with zero visibility.

As we climbed to 2500 feet on an eastward heading I could see the clouds ahead but was still denying the reality that they would impact our flight. Closer and closer we flew as Rick sat silent in the co-pilot's seat. I was suspicious of his quietness but had learned to accept it as part of my training, since he often did so just to see how I would respond. I remind you of his statement during my introductory flight, *"I could save us ten times before we hit the ground."* I was not worried in the least.

His presence in the plane outweighed
the silence in my ears.

This was the first time I'd been forced to be the decision maker in a life-and-death situation. I watched as the clouds loomed closer, but by the time I had decided I would not be able to get under them, I was too close to avoid them. In one second we went from visibility to zero visibility. Nothing Rick could have told me about flying into the clouds, could have prepared me for that moment. Suddenly I had no horizontal reference. My mind and my eyes did not agree. It was like being inside a milk jug. My first time in the clouds demonstrated effectively the reason why nearly 85% of weather-related accidents involve non-instrument rated pilots. "In a 1954 study of a 180-degree-turn experiment, the University of Illinois Institute of Aviation found that 19 out of 20 non-instrument-rated subject pilots went into a graveyard spiral soon after entering simulated instrument conditions. The 20th pilot also lost control of his aircraft, but in another maneuver. The average time between onset of instrument conditions and loss of control was 178 seconds." (reference - Wikipedia - Spacial Disorientation)

Think about that! In just under three minutes, 20 non-instrument rated pilots lost control in the clouds. They were attempting to do the very maneuver I was about to attempt. A

180-degree turn is the text book solution and only exit strategy for inadvertently entering the clouds, yet most pilots untrained in flying by instruments cannot do it. Rick was there to save me that day and had perfectly planned the lesson. No text book could have taught me what that flight illustrated to me. In life we must take the words of Jesus seriously and at face value, "However, when He, the Spirit of truth, has come, He will guide you into all truth; for He will not speak on His own authority, but whatever He hears He will speak; and He will tell you things to come." John 16:13 NKJV We all need an instructor and guide to navigate life. The presence of the Holy Spirit is stronger than the silence screaming at you. Trust Him to take control when your situation is beyond control. The song, "Jesus Take the Wheel," from Carrie Underwood is a profound truth about His ability to navigate in your life. You may need to surrender the controls before you take your flight past the point of no return. As quickly as it started, it ended. Suddenly I was in the clear and we flew safely back to Tuscaloosa airport. That lesson still resonates in my mind today. Now I'm an instrument rated pilot and have flown many hours in the clouds but I still exercise great caution and care when doing so.

As the engine of the plane roared to life and ground control cleared me to taxi, I knew this flight would not involve such dangerous procedures and it would elevate me to a new level as a pilot. Heretofore my furthest trip away from home alone had been to outlying airports like Greensboro, Reform, and Alice, all of which are small cities in Alabama and near Tuscaloosa. I had called my parents in Camden, TN and informed them of my trip and they were excited to meet me at the Camden airport.

With no fanfare or drama, my flight got underway and I began navigating towards KMSL, Muscle Shoals, AL. This first leg of my journey would take me 91 nautical miles and one hour to complete. The notes from my log book which I wrote after the flight said, "Low clouds, flew at 2500 feet, 25 knot headwind."

Because I was flying at 2500 feet I was feeling a lot of turbulence in my ride to Muscle Shoals. I kept reminding myself of what Rick had told me, "Just think of it as a rough road you're driving on. The plane won't fall out of the sky just because you hit a pot hole." Don't let a rough ride stop you from doing the thing you always wanted to do. Even if it wasn't smooth sailing, I was still going to get to Muscle Shoals and I would be there just the same as if the flight had been smooth.

This first leg required me to use pilotage and dead reckoning as my primary method of navigation. I had been trained to find landmarks along my flight path which were clearly marked on the map and fairly easy to find from the air (i.e., a river, lake, road, town, railroad, etc.) By comparing the side of the waypoint I was on to the one depicted on my chart, I could make adjustments to my heading as needed. For example: If the straight-line I'd drawn on the chart between Tuscaloosa and Muscle Shoals showed a lake to the left of my course, but when I passed it I was on the right side of the lake, I would know I wasn't correcting enough for the wind. Using that information I could correct a little more and then check the next waypoint to see how I was progressing. Can you see how important making frequent check points is? If I don't check my progress regularly, I could be so far off course by the time I do check, that identifiable waypoints elude me. People who have no checks and balances in their lives are living dangerously. You will never drift to your destiny. It is a journey of intentionality and usually involves mentors, teachers, instructors, coaches and an array of supporting characters. No quarterback wins a national championship alone. There are people all around him that make the win possible. I tell all the young men I mentor what one of my mentors, Eddie Mitchell, told me.

"You need a Paul, a Jonathan and a Timothy in your life. Paul is your mentor. Jonathan is your friend and Timothy is a son you're mentoring."

As I continued along my journey and waypoints passed beneath my wings my confidence grew. I made the adjustments needed at each waypoint and continued finding one after another until finally, I could see Muscle Shoals on the horizon. An interesting thing happened to me when landing that I've not recounted publicly very often, if at all. Here's my landing story.

After checking the surface winds I made the decision to land on runway 30. Muscle Shoals has two runways 36/18 and 30/12. I was a little west (left) of the airport as I began my downwind leg, base leg, then turned final approach. I transmitted each of the appropriate calls on the proper radio frequency. As I made my final approach, announcing my intentions to land on 30, I saw something I couldn't believe: In huge white numbers painted on the runway were the numbers 36. I was on the wrong runway! What's worse, anyone flying near the airport would have thought that I was in a different place than I actually was. This is why it's called practice and a license is really just a license to learn. It's also why pilots check their surroundings often and thoroughly when flying at any non-towered airports: Some student pilot may be announcing one thing while doing something else. Did you ever find yourself lining up on the wrong runway? Maybe you stood in the wrong line somewhere? Well, how would you like to get to Heaven only to find out that their records had you listed as an amazing athlete, a missionary that led thousands to Christ, a successful business owner that gave millions to missions or a housewife that raised a U.S. president? Be sure that the line you're standing in or the runway you're lining up to land on, is the same one Heaven has you on. "…Thy will be done, in earth as it is in heaven…" (Quote from the Lord's prayer) Nothing is more disappointing than climbing the ladder of success only to find it was leaning against the wrong wall.

COCKPIT LESSON

Make sure the numbers on the runway you're lining up on match the ones you're announcing your intentions for.

I quickly and quietly adjusted my position and made a safe landing. I never said anything about it to anyone inside the FBO and no one asked me if I had become confused. I got a signature in my log book, gassed up the plane and continued on my journey. The lesson learned in the cockpit: Make sure the numbers on the runway you're lining up on match the ones you're announcing your intentions for.

From Muscle Shoals, AL to Camden, TN the skies had cleared and I was able to climb higher and leave the turbulence behind. It is a similar flight of about 80 nautical miles, but contained a waypoint difficult to miss. The Tennessee River and Kentucky Lake combine to make an imposing figure from the air. All I had to do was keep them on the horizon off my right wing and I couldn't miss. There is a city water tower just north of the Camden air field. All I had to do was fly north until I crossed Interstate 40, which cut an east and west swath across my flight path. After that, I located highway 641 north, which ran directly past the airport. I distinctly remember entering a left downwind for runway 4, doing my midfield check-up mantra, fuel, mixture, carb-heat, and thinking to myself. "I've got to make this a good landing because my mom and dad are watching me." As I taxied to the FBO for another signature in my log book and a pat on the back from my parents, I felt as though I had just landed on the moon or some distant planet. I was doing what less than 2% of the U.S. population could do; Pilot an airplane.

After having a birthday lunch with my parents—the first one Pam had missed in our 22 years of marriage—I prepared for my flight home. A solo license is just that: You cannot bring a non-licensed person along unless a flight instructor is with you, and it was a solo cross-country flight so...Pam was waiting at home with a second birthday celebration.

The Return

I departed Camden to blue skies and light winds and flew the 20 miles to Parsons, TN for a brief visit with my brother and another signature in my flight log book. The attendant there was a flight instructor and signed my log book including his license number. He congratulated me on my long cross country and encouraged me to keep up the good work. We all need encouragement along the way and it often comes from unexpected places. Of all the places I had landed that day, Scott Field in Parsons, TN was not the place I expected to encounter a flight instructor. That airport closed only a few years later and is now only a distant memory, but I have made more than one visit to that little place tucked inside a small town community. A larger more spacious airport was built in Lexington, TN to replace Scott

Field. I've landed there several times through the years and they've maintained that same small-town airport camaraderie.

Leaving Parsons and bound for home, not only was my airplane flying high, but so was my confidence. The clouds that had kept me low on the flight up to Camden were now gone and I was being pushed now by that same wind I had fought before. Waypoints were passing faster now and the ride was smooth and enjoyable. As a part of my cross-country flight Rick had required me to use a VOR as a part of my navigational tools. From 80 miles north of Tuscaloosa I began tracking the Crimson VOR and was less reliant upon waypoints. A VOR is a VHF omnidirectional radio signal which an aircraft can tune in to using a special onboard radio to acquire a direct track of flight. There are hundreds of VORs across the U.S. and they were, at one time, the primary navigational tool used by all airlines and by any aircraft flying on an IFR flight plan. Depending upon your altitude, a VOR signal can be tracked as much as 100 miles away. Once you tune in the frequency, you simply keep the needle of an omni bearing selector in the middle and it will take you directly to the VOR. The Crimson VOR is located just four miles from the Tuscaloosa airport and I knew that if I kept the needle centered, I would fly right to the airport. Wouldn't you love to have a spiritual VOR which you could track through storms and rough flying? Well you do, sort of.

---

*The Holy Spirit's presence in
our lives gives us a built-in homing device
which we can trust to get us back on course.*

He is always pulling on our hearts and leading us in His direction. Our job is to tune in to His frequency. Unless dialed in, the needle sits idle and no signal is received.

So comfortable was I on this final leg of the flight, I didn't pay enough attention to what I was doing and did something that put my heart in my throat. Here's that short story.

Riding along at 3500 feet, I was enjoying the tailwind pushing me and counting the waypoints I passed. It suddenly occurred to me that it was time to pull on the carburetor heat. Carburetor heat is designed to eliminate potential ice building up the carburetor of a normally aspirated gas engine. This is a phenomenon which can occur any time there is high humidity in the air, even if the temperature is nowhere near freezing.

Sitting in the cockpit enjoying the relatively smooth ride I confidently reached up and pulled the carburetor heat knob to its fully open position. I gasped when in about two seconds the motor died. Talk about raising the pucker factor, I was stunned. Here I was, a low-time pilot on my solo cross-country trek in an engine out situation. Almost as quickly as I had pulled the knob, after I caught my breath, I pushed it back in and the motor restarted itself. As I took a better look I realized my mistake. In the over-confident moment of easy flying, I had mistakenly pulled the mixture knob to its off position, cutting off all gas to the engine. It's the way you shut down an airplane motor (normally done on the ground sitting on the ramp). I had forgotten a very important rule which Rick stressed to me and would later re-emphasize. What is that rule? Simply put, "Touch and identify." You should put your hand on the knob, button or lever and identify it, confirming that you have the correct one. In my case, if I had done that, I would quickly have seen that the mixture knob is RED. The carb-heat knob is black. There can be no mistaking the two. Have you ever mistaken a path you *weren't* supposed to take for one you *were* supposed to take? If we take the time to pray over our decisions and ask God for His help, He is faithful and just, helping us to make the right choices. I tell people all the time, "God won't let you miss Him if you're trying to find Him." When people say to me, "What if I miss Him?" I often quote someone unknown who first said, "He's too big to miss!" He wants to help you identify His plan for your life.

He's not trying to hide His plan from you,
He's trying to hide you in His plan.

"For in the time of trouble He shall hide me in His pavilion; In the secret place of His tabernacle He shall hide me; He shall set me high upon a rock." Psalms 27:5 NKJV

With that last small piece of drama behind me, I continued on my journey toward Tuscaloosa. When the airport came into view for me, I felt like a true pilot. I had completed the most difficult part of my training to date. There had been some tears, some fears and a lot of triumph that day. It was nearing sunset when the wheels of N5082G barked their protest as they made a smooth landing on runway 22. I taxied to Bama Air and followed the lineman to the customary spot and parked the plane. When I pulled the red mixture knob this time, it was with confidence that I had the right one. As the propeller stopped spinning and I removed my headset I knew, from this day forward, The *sky's the limit* for me.

CHAPTER 6

CHECK RIDE

A check ride is the term used in the aviation community for any type of actual flight examination. Compare a check ride to the final exam you might take before graduating from a college course. Each flight rating you acquire will end in a check ride given by an FAA flight examiner. It is a very intimidating event because that examiner has your pass or fail within his reach. Speaking of my examiner, I remember Rick telling me, "If you have the knowledge in you, Ray Ledbetter will get it out of you." *Well,* I knew the information, but to pass the check ride and get my license, it was my responsibility to convert knowledge into answers. I had seven months of training to be responsible for; it is no easy accomplishment to pass any test, since you have to assemble all the information you've learned into a logical answer when called upon. Why are we surprised to find that we are also tested by Jesus? Do you remember the story in the Bible when Jesus fed 5000 people with five loaves and two fish? In that story there is an interesting side remark that John makes, "Then Jesus lifted up His eyes, and seeing a great multitude coming toward Him, He said to Philip, "Where shall we buy bread, that these may eat?" But this He said to *test him,* for He Himself knew what He would do." John 6:5-6 *NKJV* (Italics mine)

A check ride is not guess-work for the examiner. There is a Practical Test Standard which you are required to meet. Every phase of the examination requires that the applicant be within the margins of tolerance. For example: In completing a power off stall, the examiner will require the pilot to demonstrate that the airplane can be safely recovered after entering a complete stall, and returned to normal flight. This is just one of dozens of practical test standards that must be met.

A test is the only way for a teacher to assess whether you've learned the information being taught. I've learned through a lifetime of ministry that

we are only teachers if someone else is learning.

I underwent hours of intensive mock testing from Rick. He would drill me over and over on the answers until they flowed easily from me. I went into the big event with the knowledge that Rick had never had a potential pilot fail the check ride and he had literally prepped scores of them. Why is this such a serious test? Rick drilled it into my head over and over saying, "Because the unsuspecting public deserves your best. They are going to get in an airplane to ride with you and trust you to know your stuff. There can be no shortcuts which compromise their safety." Repeatedly he told me, "If you break this rule, which one will break next?" So ingrained into me was his training, that on one occasion, after I had been a pilot for several years and had many hundreds of hours of flight time, I once refused to take a friend flying until I had been home and got a checklist that I'd forgotten. We had already sat down in the airplane and I could have easily performed the flight without the checklist, but my instructor was screaming in my head, "If you break this rule, which one will you break next?" We all need convictions that are firmly established, and on which we are unwilling to compromise.

We're only as strong as the level to which we are willing to compromise a conviction.

There are many components to a final check ride and licensing of a pilot. Not the least of these is a completed written knowledge test with a satisfactory score of 70% or more. That written test was definitely the hardest I had ever taken, but it had to be completed before I could take my check ride. While the check ride was designed to pull out the skills and training I had acquired, the written test was designed to expose the unqualified candidate. This test is not written by pilots but by test givers. It's primary function is not to pass you, but to eliminate you. There are no special concessions made if you check the wrong box on an answer. It's black and white, right or wrong. You don't get to pet a pony if you're feeling conflicted or lie down for a nap if you feel overloaded. Whether you get 70% or 100% makes 0% difference. It's pass or fail. Oh, and before I forget to mention it, a price has to be paid for both the written and the practical test. Why mention all of this? Because unlike what some of today's feel-good philosophy preachers may tell you, there is a final check ride coming for all of us. There is a written practical test standard which must be met. It was written in red and hung for all to read. It's easy to find, a cross marks the spot. There was a price paid for you and me to pass this final exam. It's either pass or fail, there is no in between. The only passing grade comes from accepting the examiner's invitation to success. To deny Him entrance into your heart and life is to blatantly and defiantly fail because of your refusal to meet the practical test standards. Jesus Christ, He is not a way, He is the only way.

As the weeks and months passed, I became more and more confident in both the airplane I was flying and my ability to fly it. I was no longer afraid it would fall out of the sky when I made a turn. Remember my earlier and prevailing fear wasn't of flying, but in doing it alone. I had 55.6 hours of total flight time when I took my check ride. I was nervous but confident.

The airplane I'd been training in for six months had become like a dear friend to me. N5082G was the tail number I'd become adept at rattling off when Tuscaloosa Tower called me on the radio. I was accustomed to the sound of the engine and the instrument panel in front of me. I knew where every gauge, switch and button were located. For six months she and I had bonded and I was comfortable in the way she felt in a stall. The contour of the controls in my hands and the ease in which she rolled down the runway for take-offs and landings had built my confidence. This was the airplane I had soloed in and the one Rick and I had slain the dragon at Greensboro in. On the day I was to begin my check ride prep work, I arrived at the airport to the news that N5082G was no longer available. It had been sent to another airport to be used there as a rental. I would now be using N2447S. This was also a Cessna 172n, but felt a little like a first date after you had been dating someone else. Some of the switches and buttons were in different locations. The panel looked familiar but not the same and the controls didn't feel like home. Then there were the different numbers used in figuring weight and balance, not to mention listening for a different tail number which, in the midst of finalizing my training, added even more pressure. It was only a month before the check ride and now I was being forced into learning another airplane. Rick's confidence was quietly contagious as we took our seat in the new bird. He helped me familiarize myself with a new cockpit. We had worked through a weight and balance equation as I took in my new surroundings.

Here's another lesson from the cockpit: Nothing lasts forever. Change is inevitable. How well you handle change will determine how well you do in life. Navigating this moment would set the stage for me in my future missional endeavors. It would create in me the phrase that I've built both a ministry and a philosophy for life upon. Every person I've taken on a missions trip for nearly two decades has heard me say "The operative word is flexible." Learning to be flexible has kept me from crashing over and over again. I'm not talking about being flexible in the absolutes, but in the things that don't really matter. You see, all Cessna 172n's use the same POH (Pilot's Operating Handbook) and respond basically the same to pilot input. The adjustments are small ones and can be easily made by the pilot. To a student pilot, a different airplane may seem like a major change. However, the manufacturer has designed them all using the same template. If you use the same template to build something, they will all turn out the same.

COCKPIT LESSON

Nothing lasts forever. Change is inevitable. How well you handle change will determine how well you do in life.

Conversely, as a carpenter I know that when cutting rafters for a building I cannot use the last one I cut as a pattern for the next one. To do so ensures that by the time I reach the end of the house, the rafters will no longer fit. If multiple cuts of any length are needed there are two options. 1) Measure each one and cut to custom length. 2) Measure and cut a pattern, then use it to mark all the rest. That's what God did. Jesus is our pattern; God did not use a man. He used Himself. If we measure everything we do by His template, we will successfully navigate anything we face.

Once past the hurdle of a different airplane, I prepared myself for the check ride by flying it as often as was practical. The first time I flew it alone was another mile marker for me. I remember flying to KGTR (Golden Triangle) airport for a required short cross country. Golden Triangle is close to Columbus Air Force Base and had, at that time, a temporary tower to coordinate training traffic from the base. As I was on final approach to land, the tower called and said, "N2447S confirm landing gear down and locked." This was standard language to the Air Force traffic he was controlling, but to a young student pilot this was disconcerting. I thought, "Does this airplane have retractable gear and I forgot? Has something happened to my landing gear that he sees but I don't?" Of course I knew that this airplane didn't have retracts, but I remember looking out the pilot's window and then leaning over to see the co-pilot's side. I confirmed that both landing gear were down and replied, "N2447S, they are down, locked and welded." He gave a chuckle and said, "Sorry about that I am used to saying that to everyone."

Here's an interesting side note that's worth mentioning. Just as suddenly as that first airplane disappeared, one day, amazingly, it reappeared and I was able to complete my check ride in the same airplane I'd begun this journey in. However, the lesson of flexibility was indelibly imprinted upon me. Since I'm a creature of habit and do not enjoy change, it was a lesson I needed to learn.

After meeting Ray Ledbetter at Bama Air we completed an hour-and-a-half oral examination, which included showing him my proposed cross country flight, complete with weight and balance, fuel reserves, and wind corrections. I breathed a sigh of relief when he suggested we make our way outside to the airplane. This was where the practical test began. As I completed the outside preflight inspection of the airplane, he quietly—and unnoticed, I might add—reached inside and turned the fuel selector to the off position. A Cessna 172 airplane has a fuel control valve with LEFT, RIGHT and BOTH settings. The normal position is the BOTH position and I had been watching for anything he might do to test the thoroughness of my preflight inspection. He was impressed, after we both sat down in the airplane, to notice I had already moved the switch to the BOTH setting. Once seated he mentioned to me, "I see you found the fuel selector knob I moved. Good job!" It set the tone for the remainder of the check ride. If I'd have missed it, I would have failed before we left the ramp. Isn't that just like people you've seen? They fail in something before they even get airborne. Being attentive and following a check list are keys to success. Make a check list and follow it. This will help keep you on track when distractions abound.

Once airborne from Tuscaloosa I was told by the examiner to fly my proposed course. I turned to the heading I had plotted and begin locating waypoints just as I'd done on my solo cross country. True to the predictions from Rick, the examiner allowed me to get on course, identify a couple of waypoints demonstrating pilotage competence, and then he canceled my flight plan stating that I had satisfied his need to know. At that point the check ride became a routine of following instructions and demonstrating my ability to perform the maneuvers he requested.

There is a part of the check ride called "unusual attitude recovery." The examiner makes the student put their head down, cover their eyes, and surrender control to him. He then puts the airplane through a series of steep banks, climbs, and descents before returning the controls to the student with the airplane in an unusual attitude and in immediate need of recovery. This means that a looming catastrophic event must be avoided, and that a perilous condition exists. The student has about two seconds in which to survey the primary flight instruments; the airspeed indicator, attitude indicator, vertical speed indicator and altimeter, then make the necessary adjustments to the situation, which is frequently an impending stall. Sometimes it's not a stall but a decent nearing the speed limitation of the aircraft. Either scenario is designed to replicate a true-to-life flight emergency. We often find ourselves in similar situations in life, where we have surrendered control to someone else and they have flown our life into the clouds and led us into an unusual attitude. It is our ability to survey the absolutes in the cockpit which will determine the outcome of our life.

The instruments in the panel
do not reflect feelings,
they only report conditions.

They are unable to correct the problem by themselves; they simply show us if we are responding correctly. It is during our times of crisis that we must trust the absolutes we have put around ourselves, in order to provide us with a roadmap to safety. We cannot react according to our feelings or fly by the seat of our pants. Look at the attitude indicator, check the vertical speed indicator to see quickly if we are in a climb or a decent.

Respond, don't react.
Reactions will crash you;
responses will save you.

Allow me to add this caveat to the entire process: It is the examiner who puts the student in this unusual attitude and it is the examiner who sits quietly waiting for the student to respond. If the student doesn't respond in the appropriate manner, the examiner says, "I have the controls," and corrects the looming dangerous situation. Upon hearing those words, the student has been previously instructed to surrender control of the aircraft to the examiner. This is just what God does for us. He gives us time to demonstrate our training by responding correctly to the information provided by the instruments, but He takes control before a crash can occur. If the examiner has to make that statement, "I have the controls," and correct the student's response, the student fails the check ride and must repeat that part of the test at another time. In the same way, some of us have been hanging around the airport retaking the same test over and over again. It's time to respond correctly and move on to the assignment for our life.

I was consumed with completing each maneuver to the very best of my ability. I was surprised when the examiner said, "Take us back to the airport." The one-hour-fifteen-minute check ride passed more quickly than I thought possible. As I made my final landing I was careful to make it a good one. As we rolled down the runway toward Bama Air, my eyes filled with tears of joy when the examiner reached out his hand and said, "Congratulations, you're the newest private pilot in the U.S." His signature in my log book and on my temporary private pilot license completed the process. I had my license and a feeling of accomplishment gushed over me like nothing I'd ever felt before or since. That temporary license has long been supplanted by a permanent version, but it has its home taped in the front of my original log book. I look at it with fondness from time to time and remember the investment it took to earn it. I remember what Zoyie Jackson, a U.S. Army First Sergeant recently told me as Pam and I were interviewing her for our radio broadcast. I had asked her about being given the

Congressional Medal of Honor, to which she quickly corrected me, "It wasn't given to me," she stated, "I earned it." The same can be said of every licensed pilot. This was not a concession which was handed to them, it was an honor they earned.

The sky is the limit to where this honor can take us, but beyond the sky is a far greater honor for those who have accepted Jesus as Lord. A crown of life, which He has purchased for us, will be given to all those who follow Him. His name is Jesus. Because of Him, the sky is not our limit.

CHAPTER 7

A LICENSE TO LEARN

In the aviation world it's called "Getting your ticket," this license I had earned. I was beyond excited to finally possess something I'd dreamed of for so long. Less than 2% of the U.S. population has a pilot's license. Since the time I had been a young evangelist, working in my first assignment in Louisiana, I had dreamed of the day I would be able to travel in an airplane. I remember being in Livingston, LA and the pastor of the church I was preaching in was a pilot. Pastor Bobby Gardner took me flying while I was there and I was hooked. This wasn't the first time I'd been in a plane; it was the second. From that day forward it was one of those things I had put on my radar, of which I said, "I'm gonna do that someday." Now that I had it, what was I going to do with it?

I got my ticket on March 21, 2003 and I spent most of that spring and summer just going to the airport and renting good ole N5082G and flying around the area. It was like being born again every time the wheels left the ground. On May 11, 2003 I fulfilled my last Sunday at the church I was working at as worship pastor. I had tendered my resignation before my check ride, knowing changes were coming our way. I had committed to that job for two years. That commitment was fulfilled on the first Sunday of May 2003. I didn't know what the future held, but I knew who held it and I was moving in His direction. I was destined for mission work and somehow I knew that flying would be a part of that.

Unemployed and uncertain, Pam and I had purchased an investment property and worked on it together all that summer and fall in the hope of flipping it for a profit. We were hoping to move from Tuscaloosa and actually drove west as far as San Antonio, Texas, looking for a potential place to relocate. We thought the closer to the border of Mexico the better. West Texas summers are one of the hottest places to be in the U.S. I remember driving toward the distant horizon as we crossed the scorched state thinking, "We fought the Mexicans for this?" It became apparent to both Pam and me during that trip that, although in many ways Texas suited our love of the western lifestyle, it just wasn't the place for us at that time.

I remember arriving in San Antonio with the air-conditioning not working in our car. After leaving over $1000.00 at a Firestone Tire Store to repair it, we decided that would be the last money Texas would get from us for the time being, and headed home. For the present, it appeared we were going to stay in Tuscaloosa.

Having made that decision, we finished remodeling the property we had purchased, and put it up for sale. As fall approached that year, I began to consider buying an airplane. As I prayed, investigated, and considered the idea, I decided I just couldn't take that financial risk. After several days of prayerful consideration, I told Pam, "We're not buying an airplane." When I awoke early the next morning I went to my customary place of prayer. It was a rocking chair on the back porch of our home. I rocked and prayed as I did every day and then God rocked me with a question,

*"Do you want to fly or drive in your ministry?
I'll pay for either one you choose; you decide and
never doubt me again about this!"*

I said "Lord I want to fly." I felt strongly that we had to reconsider the vetoed possibility of buying an airplane, and asked God to speak to Pam as well. I did not say anything to her about the way I was feeling, but later that day, after the mail arrived, she walked into my office and sailed a magazine across the room and onto my desk and said, "Go get your airplane!" On the front of that *Voice of Victory* magazine was a picture of a beautiful airplane climbing over the mountains with the caption, *"God's Got You Covered."* She, too, had been unable to shake the idea that we'd made a wrong decision the day before. When the magazine from

Kenneth Copeland arrived in the afternoon mail, we felt it was more than coincidence.

That picture from the cover of *The Voice of Victory* magazine is framed and hanging on my office wall today. It serves as a reminder to me of the words He spoke to me in the fall of 2003. Let me add this: He has done it. In all the years of owning an airplane He's had us covered. We have never paid a single cent for any of the annual inspections, which are required to be done every year on every airplane in order to maintain airworthiness. Since the first annual, in 2004, God has paid for all repairs, maintenance and travel expenses just as He promised. He has brought two aviation experts into our ministry who have done the inspections and repairs at no charge. They have often even paid for the parts. The first was Doug Vaubel, whom we met at a missions conference in Cold Water, Alabama. The second was John Hudson, of Grace Aviation, from Kingstree, SC. John was also a Pastor at the time we met and now, even though retired, he and his wife Cheryl are still a part of our ministry. At the time of writing, they are still doing the annual inspection each year. For the past two years they have traveled to our home airport to inspect and repair the plane. This year, we will return to Kingstree for the inspection and a ministry appointment.

We have flown our small plane to Mexico more times than I can count and to more appointments across the United States than anyone would have thought possible in a Piper Archer II. At the time of this writing, I have personally put over 1850 hours of flight time behind its controls. I have flown that little airplane as far north as Gillette, WY and south as far as Naples Florida. We've flown from the North Carolina coastline of Myrtle Beach to the west coast Mountains of Durango, MX and hundreds of destinations in between. N30230 has been a faithful tool for this ministry. I have filled it with people and presents for Mexican children, and I have flown in both good and bad conditions. It has carried us to the front lines of the battle and we have been blessed to have it in our arsenal of weapons. It has helped us rescue the perishing for nearly two decades and waits in the hanger for its next mission.

With the purchase of N30230, flying got serious for us. I had approximately 75 total time hours when Pam climbed aboard with me and we headed to the Mexican border for the first time. We had purchased the airplane early in October of 2003 and made one trip in it before that first trip to Mexico (more about that trip later). We flew it to the same home town airport in Camden, TN, which I had flown to in my solo cross-country. Staying true to my training, I plotted my course on sectional charts, which I used for navigational confirmation, but this airplane had an IFR-approved GPS mounted in the panel. This was navigation for dummies. All I had to do was enter the airport identifier and push the "Direct To" button.

Danger

Most of us pass danger every day but don't realize just how close it is. For example: When you're driving along in your car and meet oncoming traffic, you're passing close to danger. If either vehicle swerves just two feet across the center line, the realization of danger would no longer go unnoticed. Each time you plug in an electric device you're within inches of a dangerous charge of electricity. Every time you put gas in your car, you're only a spark away from a violently explosive and combustible product. Danger is all around us, but we frequently overlook it.

Such was the night of December 27, 2003. It was only three months after buying the airplane and we had only made one trip to Mexico and a few short flights in it. I had about 130 hours of total flight time. We had flown to Hattiesburg, MS on Christmas Day to visit Pam's family, and had now flown to Camden, TN for Christmas with my family. Both of our daughters had gone on both trips and by now I was *feeling* like a "pilot" even if I had very low time. Early in that December, the attitude indicator (AI) had malfunctioned. This is the instrument in the airplane panel which provides information about the attitude configuration of an aircraft, i.e., whether it's climbing, descending, or banking. When the AI had malfunctioned, I remember having asked Rick whether it would be ok to fly without it since I was only flying in visual conditions anyway. His answer was clear, "As you know, you only use the attitude indicator in situations where you're not able to look outside the cockpit and see the horizon. Some night, even in VFR conditions, you will depart from some black hole in the middle of nowhere and you will need that AI to maintain control of the airplane. No! You may not fly without it!" I knew he was right and had it replaced earlier that month. Doug Vaubel, our friend and mechanic at the time, had done the work.

We had arrived in Camden that afternoon to strong winds, and my concerns about the following day prompted me to call for a weather briefing early that evening. My first mistake was calling Flight Service within earshot of my wife and children. (Something that I avoided afterward for several years.) They heard me say the phrase "moderate turbulence," and began to question me. There was a prediction the following day of moderate turbulence and wind sheer (all of which sound terribly dangerous to the untrained ear). Certainly these conditions deserve consideration in flight planning, but after many hundreds of hours they've come to sound less ominous. However, for the purpose of this story let me say that I should have trusted my instincts and waited for morning. But, with the pleading from the entire family, I decided we would fly home that night, rather than risk not being able to return the following day. It was a beautiful evening, with no significant surface winds so why not go ahead and fly home? I had experience in night flight. We had, after all, just flown home at night from Pam's father's house only a night or two before. As we drove to the airport, the talk was light hearted and jovial and the girls were giddy to be getting home in a couple of hours and avoiding *turbulence* the next day.

As a studious pilot, I did all my pre-flight inspections on the aircraft while the family made their last trips to the bathroom. We said our goodbyes to Mom and Dad and then, with little fanfare or apprehension, everyone took their seat and I started the engine. The single taxi/landing light shone brightly as we left the ramp area and taxied to the run-up area at the end of the runway. There was still no real concern or apprehension inside of me. I was, after all, among the tiny percentage of Americans with a pilot's license. Besides, I had 20 hours of logged night flight: What was there to be concerned about?

I followed the check list, as always, to the letter. After the run-up, to confirm that both magnetos were functioning properly and that all gauges and instruments were within the green, I taxied into position, pushed the throttle to the firewall, and began rolling down runway 22 at Camden, TN. Still oblivious to what was awaiting me, I pulled back on the yoke and watched the nose of the airplane rise toward the skyline. It was at that moment my heart jumped into my throat: There was no skyline. It was pitch black. There was nothing to observe, no sight picture to remember. I was in a black hole, and my family was in it with me. It was at that moment I heard Rick in my head, "Some night, even in VFR conditions, you will depart from some black hole in the middle of nowhere, and you will need that AI to maintain control of the airplane. No you may not fly without it!" In about a half second, and with my heart in my throat, I switched my view from the outside of the airplane to that new attitude indicator sitting in the panel. I had never been so thankful for anything in my life. Because it doesn't know whether the airplane is in the dark, in the clouds or in clear sunshine, I could follow it and it would lead me to safety.

Camden, TN airport sits on the southeast side of town and because we had departed to the southwest on runway 22, it was a black hole. Trees line both sides of the runway, blocking out the surrounding lights. On December 27, 2003 the moon phase was only a 4% waxing crescent, meaning it was an almost moonless night which added to the darkness. By the time we had climbed to 500 ft MSL, I could see lights on the ground and could distinguish a skyline. As my eyes became more and more accustomed to the dark, I began to relax. It was then that I assessed the risk I had taken with my family. I realized then that this pilot's license I held was really just a license to learn. It only indicated that I had completed the required training, not that I had all the knowledge or training I would ever need. When my daughters, Kristen and Brittney, read this account, they will remember that night but they haven't heard until now just how dangerous that decision was. It was a stark reminder to me of just how close to danger we often pass without much more than a wink as it goes by.

How many times have you launched into something only to find yourself deeper than you wanted to be? It's like the kid that jumps into the deep end of the pool thinking he can swim, only to panic when he can no longer touch the bottom. It may be true that you can swim some, but are you prepared to swim in the deep end of the pool? My adherence to training, and Rick's thorough teaching, kept us all out of disaster that night. But what if I had not listened to my instructor? Paul wrote to his spiritual son Timothy in 2 Timothy 2:15 "Study to shew thyself approved unto God, a workman that needeth not to be ashamed, rightly dividing the word of truth." *KJV*

It is true that God gives us a divine call, but our part of His divine call is our studious preparation. He takes our natural, and applies His super, to give us supernatural results. In order to survive those difficult seasons in your life, you will need to exercise your license to learn. I spent approximately 55 hours getting my license, but the rest of my life is devoted to deepening my understanding of what I'm licensed to do.

As a pastor, an evangelist, a teacher or for that matter a Christian, I must continue my development beyond just the licensing stage. I should continue to study in order to enlarge my understanding. Bi-annually, I have to be reevaluated by an FAA-licensed flight Instructor in order to maintain my currency. They don't have the authority to take my license, only to approve or disapprove my right to exercise it. This protects myself and those who get in my airplane to go somewhere with me (the unsuspecting public). It is the same with those to whom we teach the gospel. People need to know that they are following someone who is supervised by another, and who is trustworthy and disciplined in their personal life, as well as in their spiritual life.

Another lesson from the cockpit from that night is this:

*Fearing the future can cause you
to make a mistake in the present.*

The next day was a beautiful day; we could have easily flown home and safely navigated any possible turbulence. I would rather face turbulence in the daylight than uncertainty in the dark.

CHAPTER 8

FIRST FLIGHT TO MEXICO

On the morning of our first departure to Mexico, October 16, 2003, we were at the airport early and loaded the plane. After the customary weather briefing and a farewell wave to our girls, we taxied out for takeoff. It was a three-hour flight to our first fuel stop, Nachitoches, LA. (pronounced Na-Ka-Dish). Little did I know at that time, we were beginning what would become a monthly flight just a couple of years later. With a planned fuel stop in Eastern Louisiana and West Texas, we flew over some of the same area we had driven just a few months before.

After the first fuel stop we flew direct to New Braunfels, TX and there, because of weather concerns, we decided to spend the night. It was our first experience with the saying, "If you've got time to spare, go by air!" We would become very familiar with that concept over the next eighteen months, until I received my instrument rating (see Chapter 9).

We awoke the following morning to a low cloud base, but with the promise of improvement by noon. I can still remember that "A-ha" moment when the cloud bases reached 2500 feet AGL and I remembered where we were.

We were in West Texas and the highest peak was the overpass on I-35.

There was nothing to fear by flying below the cloud deck at 2000 feet until we were able to get higher. Once that realization hit me, we were off again to our final destination, T65, Mid-valley Airport, Weslaco, TX. There we would rendezvous with Mike Poindexter, an experienced missionary pilot, and his wife Rosy. Mike had been working in Mexico for 25 years and was an experienced bush pilot. My good friend Danny Dubose (future LAM board member) had introduced us when Mike and Rosy had passed through Tuscaloosa a few months before.

As we bounced along at 2000 feet, Pam and I were seeing vast areas of open country with only scattered houses here and there. We were alone in the skies and for a low time pilot, I was a little apprehensive about being so far from any towns or services if trouble were to develop. The wind was against us and the going was slow. Even though we were flying low and slow, at least we were still moving.

Many times in our Christian walk we also feel alone and in rough, slow conditions. Facing a stiff headwind can be taxing, but the knowledge that you are making progress offsets the concern. It is easier to focus on our surroundings if we are low and slow, and sometimes we simply need to notice where we are. It was during this flight that we saw the area, from the air, that we had driven through a few months before. Sometimes God has to slow us down to get us to see what He *didn't* give us. We may never understand the, "why," but the important thing is to understand the "Who." God is the one who directs our paths and we must trust His judgement. He knows us better than we know ourselves. Pam and I are not flat land people. We are not dry scrub brush people. We like soil not sand. We like green grass and trees, not mesquite brush and cactus. We like rain and snow. It was during this bumpy flight that we were made keenly aware that West Texas was not our place to live, only a place to pass through.

Where Is It?

Weslaco, TX is tucked snugly between Brownsville and McAllen, TX.

We were literally right on the airport before we saw it. Mid-Valley airport, T65, lay just off the nose of the airplane and yet we were both struggling to find it. The GPS told us where to look, but we still had to find it amid interstates, city streets and a sprawling West Texas landscape. Finding an airport is not as easy as you may think. Even a mile-long runway can be hard to spot in the afternoon sun. Something else I've learned in the cockpit is this: Like an airport you can't see, sometimes you can be right on top of the will of God for your life, and still not see it. It can be glaring us in the face, but because our perception is skewed, we are often looking past the very thing we're looking for.

Pam and I were both inexperienced at finding airports in those days, but over the years we have become much better at it. In the early days we often had contests to see who could be the first to spot the airport. Once you learn to look for the environment of an airport, they're easier to find. Long before an airport comes into view, the terrain and structures reveal its possible presence. Airports are usually located in wide open spaces (except in cases like Weslaco were the city had built up all around it). Most airports have a row of hangers which sit adjacent to the runway. Knowing the runway number gives

COCKPIT LESSON

Like an airport you can't see, sometimes you can be right on top of the will of God for your life, and still not see it.

you the compass heading to associate it with. Remember something I said earlier in this book? Runway numbers correspond to compass headings with one number removed. (Example: Runway 13 at Weslaco means that it's oriented at a 130° heading) Knowing the orientation of a runway makes it easier to find. Using the directional gyro or compass, in the panel in front of you, it's easy to determine where to look. In this way you're at least looking in the right direction to find it. The landscape will also help direct your search. Just look for a large open space, a straight line of buildings, and a long paved area with huge numbers printed on it. Finding the runway is usually easy once you're looking in the right place.

We learned to stop looking for the airport and start looking for the airport environment. Once we learned to do that, our airport discoveries went up drastically. If you're struggling to find God's will for your life, try finding His environment. Be careful who you hang out with. Be picky about your friends. Stop visiting places that are not conducive to finding His will. You're not going to find His will in the wrong place. Be intent on finding His environment; from there His will becomes visible. It'll be that long paved area with big numbers written on it.

Some people wrongly think that finding an airport at night is even more difficult. I will tell you this,

---

the darker the night, the easier an airport is to find.

At night there is a beacon spinning 360° degrees which is white on one side and green on the other. In the cockpit of an airplane, at ten nautical miles, this appears like a flashing green and white light. It grabs your attention and reels you in like a fish on a line. At some larger airports with control towers, there are even lights that act as an arrow called a "rabbit" by pilots. They flash in sequence to form a trail several hundred feet long which is impossible to miss. Follow the rabbit, it will lead you to the runway.

The runway edge lights and taxi lights, which can be controlled by the pilot, are a wonderful sight from an airplane. Each airport has its own assigned radio frequency, and when dialed in, the pilot of an arriving flight can click the microphone to:

- Turn lights on by clicking 5 times within 5 seconds
- Adjust to low/medium/high by clicking 3, 5, or 7 times within 5 seconds once they're on.

If you've been looking for the will of God for your life and feel unsuccessful, why not try looking for the runway environment? If it's dark all around you, adjust your eyes outside the cockpit, look for the flashing light, then fly towards it. Remember the wise men who followed the star? They didn't even have the Holy Spirit to guide them. He's still shinning for those who will look. In our case it's not a rabbit but a dove leading us to the runway. God's Holy Spirit wants to lead you to God's plan and will for your life. Follow him, you will find the runway. (God's will)

We were almost on top of runway 13 before we saw it. (Since 2003 runway 13 has been changed to 14. This is because over time, as the Earth's magnetic field changes, runway numbers shift a tiny bit until they are actually closer to the next degree than the former.)

I made a 45° entry into the downwind and called my position to the area traffic. Mike was waiting in the lobby of the airport for our arrival. He told me later that the attendant looked at him and said, "He doesn't sound like a new pilot. He sounds like a professional!" Well, the truth is, most of us have learned to bluff our way through sometimes. While I was new at flying, I was an old hand with a microphone in my hand, and now it was paying benefits.

Be confident in your abilities
but be pliable in your deficiencies.

Durango, Mexico

We arrived at Weslaco, TX on Friday, October 17, 2003 for the very first time. It would become a place we frequented for the next two years. It was our first exposure to the south west Texas area and we enjoyed visiting South Padre Island with Mike and Rosy. We visited the old wharfs, ate seafood fresh from the Gulf of Mexico and preached at the church where Mike pastored.

I was not only a freshly minted pilot; I was also very new to the Spanish language and still made many mistakes. But, even with mistakes, people still embrace you, and the fact that you try endears you to them even more. As these people listened to our heart for missions and opened theirs us, it was an altogether great experience for Pam and me.

On Monday morning October 20, 2003 we loaded Mike's Cessna 210 and departed for Durango, MX. There was a thin layer of clouds covering the sky as we prepared to leave. "That's no problem, we have this all the time down here," Mike said, as we drove to the airport from their home. "We'll just get an IFR clearance and get on top." I was all eyes and ears. This was real life flying and I was right in the middle of it. After checking the weather to confirm what we believed—that it was only a local condition—we filed the flight plan. Having loaded the airplane, and completed the checklist, we taxied to the runway for run-up and departure. As ATC gave us the clearance we needed to climb through the overcast, it seemed like Greek to me. I was once again trusting an instructor who knew things I needed to know. Mike held many of the same credentials Rick held and, though I didn't know him well, I had to trust that he knew what he was doing. Mike had asked me to fly left seat (Something instructors usually do for a student) and I can still remember his short reprimand to me after I had accidentally turned off the Avionics kill switch, thinking I was checking the alternator charge. "Don't push any buttons without I tell you to." Those were his exact words to me. I've never forgotten those words and have even used an adaptation of them many times since. Fortunately my mistake caused no harm to the radios or any equipment, but here's another valuable lesson I learned in the cockpit that day: Wait for instructions before performing by memory, that which should be performed by a checklist. My eagerness to demonstrate my ability could have cost a lot of money. It's better to wait until asked to do something rather than to try to do it without invitation. I include Mike's teaching moment in this book to demonstrate that through our lifetime, we will have many instructors. What they teach us is their choice, what we learn from them is ours.

As Durango came into view we knew that our environment was changing again. We had flown over the sprawling cities of Monterrey and Saltillo en route to Durango, but they were far to the east from our destination. It had been years since Pam had been in Mexico and several months for me. Needless to say, we were very excited to leave that small cockpit, me for one reason, Pam for another. (A three-hour flight in an unpressurized aircraft at 12,000 feet will build pressure of a different nature.)

COCKPIT LESSON

Wait for instructions before performing by memory, that which should be performed by a checklist.

Neither of us had ever arrived at a foreign airport on a private flight, and the experience was very interesting. I had a lot to learn and God had once again strategically positioned me with a friend who would be my teacher for the next two years while I learned about flying in Mexico. The many-step procedure for arrivals and departures in Mexico, is nothing like here in the U.S. It took time, but I eventually learned the intricacies of the process.

On that first arrival we met a woman in customs (we'll call her Juanita, I can't recall her name), who was very interested in the mission Mike and Rosy had started in the outlying village of Chupaderos. (Note: Chupaderos is an old movie set built by John Wayne and used in many of the old westerns you've perhaps seen on the big screen or on a DVD. The Sons of Katie Elder, along with many other old westerns, was filmed there and at Wayne's nearby ranch. I visited the ranch on one of my many trips there and met Antonio Lozoya who now owns it. I have an old piece of pottery in my office today, and an old piece of mesquite driftwood that resembles a monkey, both of which were given to me by Antonio on that visit. He had worked for John Wayne for many years and managed the ranch for him in his absence. He inherited the ranch after the Duke's death.)

As we cleared customs and immigration that day of our first arrival, Juanita expressed an interest in our mission. I gave her a CD I had recently recorded and invited her to the service at Chupaderos. To our surprise, she and her boyfriend came to the service that night. It was an open-air service under a pavilion porch. There were only enough chairs for a few people (25-30) but many stood around the edges including Juanita and her boyfriend. They listened as this gringo preacher struggled through the delivery of his message and then, during the altar call, she raised her hand to receive Christ. This was of eternal benefit to her and temporary benefit to us. Let me explain. As a customs officer at the Durango airport, she had the power to allow or not allow things that Mike and Rosy brought in from the U.S. Often they would bring clothing in bags and suitcases to give to the people at the mission. On more than one occasion they had not been allowed to bring it into the country. After Juanita's conversion, this process went much better until she was eventually transferred to another airport. Hence the reason the benefit was only temporary in our case. In Heaven someday I will meet her again and we will celebrate the help she gave the poor people living at an old movie set in Chupaderos, Mexico.

COCKPIT LESSON

If I maintain the heading which the charts, the compass and the GPS give me, I will eventually arrive at my destination.

We were a long way from Tuscaloosa, AL - KTCL airport—about 850 nautical miles. When we departed our home base for this first flight to Mexico, we could not see the border, but here's something else I learned in the cockpit: If I maintain the heading which the charts, the compass and the GPS give me, I will eventually arrive at my destination. Many times through the years I've had to trust the indicator without any indication that it was right. The Lord once spoke to me during an early morning meeting saying, "Jim, wait for me at the corner of faith and hope. I will not be early, but neither will I be late." I wrote it down to remember it later. As with many of those meditational moments alone with Him, these words are forever etched into my memory and prayer journal. He is not trying to avoid us, He is longing to enjoy us, just as we do our children.

Life can be a lot like that. There will be seasons when you're looking for evidence, which you won't find; evidence that tells you you're going the right way, but all you really have are the coordinates which faith has given you. Keep flying to those coordinates and you'll eventually arrive at your destination. Even if you get there before Him wait, He'll be along directly.

CHAPTER 9

INSTRUMENT TRAINING

It has been said that a VFR (see glossary) pilot is half a pilot and an IFR pilot is three quarters of one, i.e., the VFR pilot can only fly about half the time due to weather interruptions, and the IFR pilot can only make about three quarters of his flights. (I'm referring to pilots who are flying at my level: single engine, single pilot aircraft.) There will still be times when you simply cannot fly due to weather interference. As my flight experiences continued to grow, more and more of our flights were cancelled, delayed and in some cases risked, due to low clouds, I knew that something had to be done about my instrument training. Now, let me be absolutely clear about this one thing: At no time during this season did I fly in the clouds nor did I take unnecessary risks, which would have threatened our lives or those who traveled with us. What I did do however, is a practice called scud running. The intent of scud running is to stay clear of clouds, even though IMC (See glossary) conditions exist and still remain safely above terrain and/or obstructions.

As 2004 arrived we were making more and more flights to speaking engagements around the south east. I was gaining hours of experience, but I was still held in check by low ceilings which an IFR-rated pilot could have flown through, got on top of the cloud deck, and avoided being grounded by a simple layer clouds.

I held a pilot's license for fifteen months before committing to the next level: Instrument rating. Simply put, this trains a pilot to fly in the clouds, and to follow an instrument approach to landing. Instrument-rated pilots are trained in recovery from unusual attitudes solely by instrument reference and commitment to absolute trust in those instruments. The need of this rating was never so apparent to me as it was on a trip I took with my oldest daughter, Kristen, in the spring of 2004.

In those days I was still working with missionary Mike Poindexter in the small movie set town of Chupaderos, Mexico. We were building a church there and I had made the trip from Tuscaloosa to the border a couple of times.

Sis (my name for her) and I left Tuscaloosa with our hopes high but our altitude low. An overcast sky kept us pinned to the deck under a layer of clouds and in an intense headwind. As we fought our way westward I kept my eye on the overcast and my running time. It became apparent that we were not going to be able to reach our planned fuel stop, and the low hanging clouds finally forced us to land at an unscheduled airport in Magee, MS. What would normally be a 1.1 hour flight had taken me 2.0 hours to complete. The winds were brutal and the bouncing was nearly unbearable for Sis. This wasn't her first flight, but she didn't have the experience I had, and I could see that we needed to wait for a break in the clouds. There is a note in my log book beside this entry which says, "Landed at Magee, MS because of low ceilings." I can assure you it wasn't just low ceilings; we could not have made my scheduled fuel stop at KLCH (Lake Charles, LA). Here's a little something I've learned in the cockpit: The fuel gauge in the panel is only for a reference, it cannot be believed. The time on the clock is the only thing that matters. Many pilots have mistaken distance for duration. They are not the same. It doesn't matter how many times you've made a trip before without stopping for fuel. All that matters is how long the engine has been running. Pilots know that distance and duration are not created equally. Allow me to explain.

COCKPIT LESSON

The fuel gauge in the panel is only for a reference, it cannot be believed. The time on the clock is the only thing that matters.

An airplane is like a boat in a river. The ground speed is all that matters when calculating an arrival time. If your boat is going upstream, the ground speed is *reduced* by whatever the speed of the current is. If you're traveling downstream, it's *increased* by the speed of the current. If your boat is going 45 MPH and the river current is 10 MPH, your actual ground speed is only 35 MPH.

Now, apply that same rule to an airplane. Even though my Piper Archer will fly at a true airspeed of 125 KTS, if the wind against me is 45 KTS (A very real scenario) I'm really only covering the ground at 80 KTS. Now apply that same equation to our flight. We were going upstream, against the current. My airplane doesn't care about the wind, the clouds, the distance, or the miles it's traveled. At altitude, on any given day, with the fuel leaned to peak performance, the fuel burn is 10 gallons per hour. There are 48 usable gallons in the tanks. It is going to run 4.8 hours and then stop running. It doesn't care where it is or if it's reached its destination. It doesn't care if it's sitting on the runway or at 10,000 feet —

Any airplane will shut down from fuel starvation. So will your spirit, man.

No respectable pilot will burn his tanks down to less than 1 hour of fuel reserve. This is a safety cushion just in case you arrive at a destination airport and can't land due to some emergency on the field and you have to divert to another airport. Minimum fuel reserves are in place and required by law for our protection, they are: 30 minutes of reserve fuel for VFR flights and 45 minutes of reserve for night flights. IFR minimums require 45 minutes day and night. I err on the side of safety. I have established an iron-fast rule: If I can't arrive in 3:45 minutes, stop somewhere for fuel.

This leaves at least 1 hour of fuel in the tanks in a worst-case scenario.

Wouldn't it benefit our spiritual walk if we would take the same precautions? By doing regular preventive maintenance and making fuel stops for your spirit man, you can avoid costly and difficult repairs. These could have been eliminated if you'd just stopped for gas.

I've read many NTSB reports which listed *fuel exhaustion* as the primary cause of the accident. In some of these cases, the pilot survived and was quoted as saying, "I've made this flight many times and without needing to stop for fuel." How foolish can anyone be? A good instructor teaches his students early on that there are two things you can never get back: 1) unused runway length, and 2) fuel you didn't buy.

I encourage you: Stop your busy life and take in the much-needed spiritual fuel you can't live without. Set a daily appointment with God and keep it. I love what Joyce Meyer says, "It's not so much about what you do there, it's that you showed up." God wants an appointment with you.

It's inconceivable that the creator of the universe wants an appointment with me, but it's not for me to understand, it's just for me to attend.

Give Him time to top off your tanks, you'll be glad you did.

More Decisions

Sis and I struggled with cloud issues all the way to the border that day. I remember at one point being over the Gulf of Mexico flying at altitudes as low as 1000 feet in order to stay well clear of clouds. That's when I made the decision, "As soon as money is available, I'm getting my instrument rating." My log book entry doesn't tell me the hour we arrived at Weslaco, TX that day, but it does contain the following entry: "Arrived tired." It was a long day, and by the time we got to Mike and Rosy's house to spend the night, we were beat. I was unsure of what the next day's flight conditions would be, but went to bed hopeful for improvement.

We awoke the next morning to low ceilings and rain in the forecast. That made the decision easy for me. There would be no flight into Mexico. We drove across the border to Progresso, and bought bus tickets to Ciudad Victoria, Mexico. Rather than a 1.5 hour flight, we spent the whole day on a Mexican bus stopping at every wide spot in the road.

Without giving you all the details of that trip, let me sum it up by saying, by the time we made it home to Tuscaloosa, I was convinced it was time to get on with my training. Here's something else I learned in the cockpit: Training really never ends. Whatever you do in life, you will need to continue to invest in yourself by requiring yourself to improve. It's like the old violinist who in his eighties who, when asked by an interviewer why he practiced so much each day replied, "You know, I think I'm getting better!"

At home I was doing any kind of handyman service work I could find in and around Tuscaloosa to make a living. We would do handyman work all week and preach every weekend that a door opened for us to do so. Keep in mind, I had been in full time ministry since 1979 and this was 2003. This was a difficult season for me, but I wanted to see LAM succeed even if it meant carrying the ministry on my back for a while. Pam and I made a trip to South Dakota to preach and had received a donation from some

COCKPIT LESSON

Training really never ends. Whatever you do in life, you will need to continue to invest in yourself by requiring yourself to improve.

dear friends, Pat & Jane Graham, for $2000.00 for LAM. I mention them by name in Pat's honor. He went home to be with the Lord on December 18, 2012. He was a blessing to our life and ministry both financially and as a neighbor and friend in South Dakota. This particular donation would give me the cash I needed to take the step to the next level of flying: That of an instrument rating. I shall always remember Pat and Jane's kindness, friendship and partnership.

Ten Days

With the money in the bank, I began looking for a flight school which offered intense training with rapid completion. To my surprise I found The Pilot Center, just an hour's flight from Tuscaloosa, in the small town of Wetumpka, AL. After getting all the details worked out, I enrolled in the ten-day immersion instrument course. Lodging was provided with the course, but was nothing more than a bed and bath in a hanger and, trust me, that's about all I had time for. From early morning until after dark I was either flying, studying, or sleeping.

COCKPIT LESSON

Landing at the wrong place could delay—if not destroy —your future.

Wetumpka airport is located just outside of Montgomery, AL and most of the instrument approaches I practiced were done there. It was good airspace to practice in because there is a lot of traffic due to Maxwell Air Force Base, which is also located in the area. In fact, my instrument instructor took great pains to make me aware of the impending danger of landing at the wrong airport. Hence yet another thing I learned in the cockpit: Landing at the wrong place could delay—if not destroy—your future. Maxwell Air Force base is not a place you want to land without a clearance. Your airplane will be surrounded by armed guards and you will be detained, if not arrested, for doing so. It is an infraction against the U.S. Air Force, and the FAA takes a dim view of those who do such things. It will be met with sharp discipline. By using an IFR approach plate you cannot land at the wrong airport. An approach plate is a road map to the airport to which it pertains. Making good decisions is the key to arriving at your destination airport.

Even if it lies near other attractive offers, your destiny holds your blessing and every decision should be made in the light of its impact upon your future.

We never know when we're making those *future-altering choices*, so always use God's approach plate found in Matthew 7:7 "Ask, and it will be given to you; seek, and you will find; knock, and it will be opened to you." *NKJV* Another one is found in James 1:5 "If any of you lacks wisdom, let him ask of God, who gives to all liberally and without reproach, and it will be given to him." *NKJV*

My experience at The Pilot Center those ten days can be best described by the old saying, "It was like drinking from a fire hydrant." Learning to aviate, navigate, and communicate without outside reference is a challenge. I was required to do all flying, except take-offs and landings, wearing a hood to shield my eyes from seeing anything outside the cockpit.

I have included a sample instrument approach plate, to help you understand just how landing is possible, even though you're unable to see the airport or the runway from the sky. (Figure 9a) I believe it will help you understand how finding your way on a cloudy day is not guess work, but very precise. It is the approach plate for my home airport in Waverly, TN (0M5). A thorough examination of it will reveal key components which are necessary for a successful landing. The approach plate shows you the altitude you need to fly in order to remain clear of any obstructions such as terrain or towers in the area. It gives you the headings to fly, the frequencies you should be tuned in to, and all other pertinent airport information. It even gives you information such as runway number, length and width.

There are three points marked IAF (initial approach fix) on the plate. After receiving a clearance from ATC (air traffic control) you fly directly to one of these GPS fixes and then you follow the headings and maintain the altitude written just above them. Once arriving at the fix marked FAF (final approach fix) the pilot can then descend to the specified altitude, which in this case is 1120 feet MSL. That altitude is in MSL so that it will match the altimeter in the airplane. For the actual distance above the ground we subtract the airport elevation of 756 feet from the MDA (minimal decent altitude), which results in 364 feet above the ground. That's the lowest you can legally descend unless you can see the runway

COCKPIT LESSON

If the runway's not where it's supposed to be, it's not wrong —you are.

environment. If you're on course, the runway will be 5.3 miles directly in front of you. It's an amazing experience to descend out of the clouds and see a runway lying exactly where it's supposed to be. Here's something else I've learned in the cockpit: If the runway's not where it's supposed to be, it's not wrong—you are.

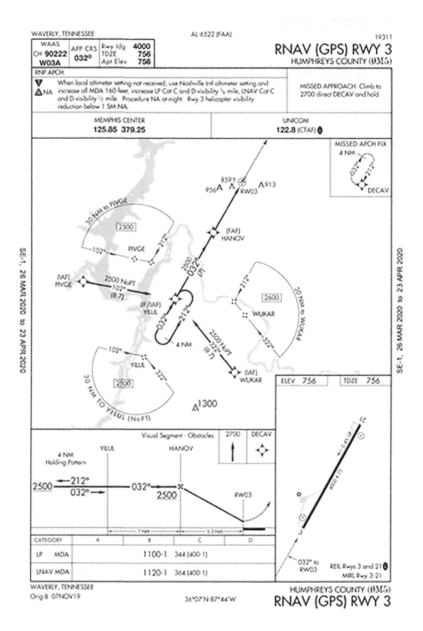

Figure 9a

Figure 9b

Figure 9c

Six Essential Instruments

There are six basic instruments in the panel of an IFR-rated airplane and they are indispensable for conducting safe flight into IMC. They are:

- Airspeed indicator
- Attitude indicator
- Altimeter
- Turn coordinator
- Directional gyro
- Vertical speed indicator

All of these instruments provide information to the pilot which allows him/her to maintain control of the airplane while in clouds or low visibility such as darkness, haze or rain. In addition to these six, there are other instruments which greatly aid in this process, but are optional equipment and are present in many modern aircraft. One of those is an IFR-rated GPS. In order to fly the approach plate shown here, an IFR-rated GPS is required. In addition, of great assistance is a moving map with geo-reference overlay, allowing your present location to be depicted on the map. I've included an example of that same approach plate with my GPS position depicted on it. I've included some screen shots taken from my iPad, as Pam and I were arriving home on a typical IFR flight plan and approach to landing. Find the small airplane in the pictures to see our location on the approach. (Figures 9b, 9c, & 9d)

Figure 9d

The heading and altitude are depicted on each leg of the approach. Even if the ground is obscured by a layer of clouds, the approach plate will line you up with the center line of the runway and allow you to descend to the specified altitude with no danger of hitting anything. The purpose of this book is not to teach you to fly, but to share things I've learned in the cockpit, and here is another: Even when the horizon is hidden and there are thick clouds all around, if I fly the approach plate as published, I will be on the centerline of the runway when I descend below the clouds.

There are literally very few things in life that compare to descending below a cloud deck and finding a runway right in front of you. God's word can be trusted just as the instruments and approach plate you're following.

A terrible crash occurred in Houston, TX, on November 22, 2004 killing everyone on board simply because the flight crew ignored their instruments. The flight, N85VT, which was a Gulfstream III, was arriving to pick up former president George Bush (Senior) for a trip to Ecuador, where he was to speak at a conference. The pilot and co-pilot had both logged more than 19,000 hours of flight time. They disagreed about their instrument settings, but rather than climb to a safe altitude and cross check them, they continued descending through a low cloud base of 100 feet AGL and very low visibility, and struck a light pole. It turned out the instruments were correct; 100 feet AGL is not the time to discuss instrument accuracy or calibration. That should always be done at a safe altitude.

COCKPIT LESSON

Even when the horizon is hidden and there are thick clouds all around, if I fly the approach plate as published, I will be on the centerline of the runway when I descend below the clouds.

At decision altitude,
in a crucial moment, your instruments
must have the deciding vote. Trust them.

In the same manner we have to trust that God is nearer than we think. He is interested in our safe landing at our destiny. Sometimes His purposes are not completely understood, yet it behooves us to follow His leading and trust His word.

CHAPTER 10

SITUATIONAL AWARENESS

We are all susceptible to distractions. In Luke 8:18 Jesus makes a really odd statement. He says, "Therefore take heed how you hear. For whoever has, to him more will be given; and whoever does not have, even what he seems to have will be taken from him." *NKJV*

Soon after making that statement, Jesus tells His disciples in verse 22 of the same chapter "Let us cross over to the other side of the lake." This sounds normal to them, but the trip to the other side is anything but normal. Along the way Jesus falls asleep and a big wind comes up. Now, keep in mind that several of these men were fisherman before they got into ministry. They had spent their lives on the water and in every conceivable weather condition, yet they are terrified to the point that they wake Jesus saying, "Master, Master, we are perishing!" *NKJV*

What had happened to His instructions: "…Take heed how you hear."? They had missed a key phrase in the briefing. He had said, *"Let us cross over to the other side of the lake."*

Jesus had already indicated to them His plan was to go over not go under.

Situational awareness is a term used by pilots and refers to cockpit awareness and resource management. I remember when I was taking my check ride, both for my private license as well as my instrument rating; asking the flight examiner to participate was well within my scope as PIC. When He tried to distract me from the assigned task, I asked him to remain quiet, to observe a *sterile cockpit*. This was all a part of the testing process. If he had been able to distract me from my tasks, I would have, at minimum, been chastised and possibly even failed. When I needed an extra hand, I asked him to hold things for me. All of this impressed him because as PIC (pilot in command) it was within my scope of authority to manage the cockpit resources, and passengers can be one of those resources.

If the men in that boat with Jesus had paid better attention during the lesson on listening and in preflight briefing, they would not have been worried about the storm and would possibly have gotten some rest along with Jesus. Something else I've learned in the cockpit:

---

*I better pay close attention
while on the land to what's going to be
happening while in the air.*

I love something my wife, Pam, pointed out to me several years ago. When Peter was in prison awaiting a death sentence, in perhaps the biggest storm of his life, he followed the example of Jesus: He was sound asleep between two guards. He seems to have learned from his time on the boat in the storm, that sleeping is better than worrying. Perhaps this is why he also got out of the boat during a storm, and walked on water to be with Jesus.

Situational awareness has been a contributing factor in many air fatalities. Whether you are flying a single-engine Piper or a jet airline, the requirement is the same. You must pay attention to the circumstances around you and focus on the tasks at hand.

To further illustrate my point, I'd like to tell you a couple of stories which I think you'll find interesting; they will drive home the point for absolute focus and situational awareness.

Comair Flight 5191

How important is situational awareness? A tragic accident occurred on Aug 27, 2006 at Lexington, KY, Blue Grass Airport, which could have been completely avoided if the pilots had paid closer attention to what they saw and heard. Per FAA regulations, they heard and read back the clearance from the Lexington ground controller. (It's also significant to point out that the ground controller was the tower controller and that, due to this accident, a two-person policy was implemented for all towers.) It was early morning at 6:07 a.m. when Captain Jeffery Clay taxied the airplane to runway 26 for departure. The flight had received a clearance to depart runway 22 for their 1:07 flight to Atlanta, GA.

The flight crew had initially boarded the wrong airplane and started its APU. (auxiliary power unit). A ramp attendant notified the flight crew members and told them that they had boarded the wrong airplane. The flight crew then shut down the APU and proceeded to the correct airplane. After receiving the flight clearance to taxi to Runway 22 for departure, Captain Jeffrey Clay taxied the aircraft to Runway 26. Not a problem? Just three numbers off? The Bombardier Jet 100ER needed 3750 feet just to rotate. (Lift the nose off the runway). Runway 26 is only 3500 ft long. Runway 22 is 7000 ft long and is the only runway at Lexington for airliner use. YOU SHOULD'T BE ABLE TO MISS IT. THERE ARE GIANT WHITE LETTERS PAINTED ON THE END THAT READ: 22

Perhaps you remember some training I introduced to you earlier in this book. Runway headings are compass headings with one digit dropped off. So runway 22 is a compass heading of 220° degrees. If he had just looked at his compass before rolling, he would have seen that something wasn't right. His compass would have been showing 260° degrees instead of 220. Question: Have you checked your compass heading with your assigned heading? It might pay to take a moment to confirm that they match.

The runaway lights were on for runway 22 but not for 26. Not only did they have to ignore that very obvious absence, they even talked about it. At a speed approaching 100 knots (120 mph), First officer James Polehinke remarked, "That is weird with no lights," referring to the lack of lighting on Runway 26—it was about an hour before daybreak. "Yeah", confirmed Captain Clay, but the flight data recorder gave no indication that either pilot tried to abort the takeoff as the aircraft accelerated to 137 knots (158 mph).

One of the saddest things I've ever read is the transcript of the cockpit voice recorder for flight 5191. It is a litany of living room conversation or back porch yarn spinning. Both Captain and First Officer were discussing job options, family issues and other topics. They were clearly not paying attention to the work at hand, nor was situational awareness being practiced. An FAA regulation requires a sterile cockpit during departure or arrival proceedings. By definition the sterile cockpit rule is: "During critical phases of flight (normally below 10,000 feet), only activities required for the safe operation of the aircraft may be carried out, and all non-essential activities in the cockpit are forbidden." ("FAR Part 121 Sec. 121.542 effective as of 04/14/2014.") This was clearly disregarded. Once again I'm reminded of something Rick Price is fond of saying, "If you're going to disregard this regulation, which one will be next?"

THE SKY'S THE LIMIT

Based upon an estimated take-off weight of 49,087 pounds the manufacturer calculated speed of 138 knots (159 miles per hour) and a distance of 3,744 feet would have been needed for rotation (increasing nose-up pitch), with even more runway needed to achieve take off.

The cockpit voice recorder confirmed that the first officer had briefed the takeoff decision speed (V1) (point of no abort) as 137 knots and the rotation speed (VR) as 142 knots. At 131 knots the captain called, "V1, rotate," and said, "whoa..." the flight data recorder showed that the callout for V1 occurred 6 knots early and that the callout for VR occurred 11 knots early; both callouts took place when the airplane was at an airspeed of 131 knots. There was no chance of flight. The doomed flight screamed off the end of the runway and sent forty-seven passengers and two flight crew into eternity.

"The National Transportation Safety Board determines the probable cause(s) of this accident to be: The flight crew members' failure to use available cues and aids to identify the airplane's location on the airport surface during taxi and their failure to cross-check and verify that the airplane was on the correct runway before takeoff. Contributing to the accident were the flight crew's non-pertinent conversation during taxi, which resulted in a loss of positional awareness." (Taken from NTSB website)

Something I've learned in the cockpit: Everyone who enters my airplane is trusting me to know what I'm doing and to do it safely, to the best of my ability. Likewise, those who are following me as a leader, are trusting me to lead with an honest heart and a sincere desire to follow God's laws.

Leadership is a serious responsibility and we who lead must approach it remembering the charge that the Apostle James gave us: "My brethren, let not many of you become teachers, knowing that we shall receive a stricter judgment." James 3:1 *NKJV*

Distractions will cause you to lose sight of your purpose and mission.

It was distraction that caused Peter to start sinking in the water he was walking on. He was distracted by the wind and waves.

Nehemiah knew the way to avoid distractions: "...I am doing a great work, so that I cannot come down. Why should the work cease while I leave it and go down to you?" Nehemiah 6:3 *NKJV*

COCKPIT LESSON

Everyone who enters my airplane is trusting me to know what I'm doing and to do it safely, to the best of my ability.

My grandfather, R.W. Stockdale, was a minister for more than 50 years and he often told me, *"Jim, you can learn from other people's mistakes."* And, *"If you meet a man who has stopped learning, stay away from him."* I've tried to live my life using that philosophy. I look forward to seeing him someday when my flight lands on the other side.

Fatal Distractions

On December 29, 1972 at 9:20 p.m., Eastern Airlines Flight 401 departed John F Kennedy Airport in Queens, NY for Miami, FL. It was a routine flight with no complications. As the aircraft arrived in Miami at 11:32 and began its approach to landing, the flight crew noticed the indicator light for the nose gear had failed to illuminate green. The captain contacted Miami tower requesting to enter a holding pattern at 2000 feet while they investigated. It's important to note that the landing gear could have been lowered manually should it have been necessary. Instead, the captain dispatched the flight engineer to the avionics bay, which is located below the flight deck, for a visual inspection. The captain and first officer manually began to disassemble the indicator light trying to ascertain if it was functioning. Being distracted by the indicator light, both failed to noticed that the altitude hold on the autopilot, had not been engaged. They broke a cardinal rule of aviation which we all learn in our initial flight training. It's acronym is A-N-C and it's the law we fly by.

- Aviate
- Navigate
- Communicate

The number one responsibility of every pilot is to fly the plane. Second is to navigate—knowing where you are and where you're going is crucial to a successful flight. Third is to communicate your intentions. If they had followed this rule, this accident could have been avoided. How many fatal distractions occur in lives every day that could be avoided? There's grace to resist every temptation if we will first fly the plane. As flight 401 continued in the oval holding pattern, with each turn and ever so slowly, it descended into the darkness over the Everglades swamp, no one noticed. It was imperceptible because of the darkness and the preoccupation of the pilots. They were fascinated with their problem solving instead of flying. The 55-year-old captain was a 32-year veteran who had logged more than 29,000 flight hours, proving that no one is immune to fatal distractions. After losing the first 250 feet of altitude, a warning alarm sounded, however the alarm was located at the flight engineer's work station: Remember, he had been dispatched to the avionics bay for a visual confirmation of the nose gear. No one was home at his desk. There was no one to hear the warning alarm, no one was flying plane, everyone was doing something else. The following conversation was taken from the cockpit flight recorder after the crash.

> Co-pilot: "We did something to the altitude."
>
> Pilot: "What?"
>
> Co-pilot: "We're still at 2000 right?"
>
> Pilot: "Hey - what's happening here?"

Ten seconds later, as the Captain of the ship noticed the discrepancy, the left wing struck the Everglades and 99 people went into eternity; two more died shortly after.

Would you believe me if I told you a fifty cent light bulb could have saved the lives of everyone on board of flight 401? The irony of it all is that the landing gear was down: The cause of the crash was ruled as pilot error due to preoccupation with a burned-out lightbulb. The pilot and co-pilot's preoccupation with a simple lightbulb, cost the lives of 101 people. When we allow distractions into our lives, no matter how innocent they may seem, they really could be quite expensive to our future and not worth the cost.

"Blow the trumpet in Zion, And sound an alarm in My holy mountain..!" Joel 2:1 *NKJV*

If everyone is doing other things, who's flying the plane? Who will hear the alarm if I am out of my place? As each one stays in their lane, does his/her job and adheres to the rules surrounding that job, we all benefit.

Jesus said, "Therefore take heed how you hear." At every airport with a control tower, communication with ground control, is absolutely required before moving any vehicle into the movement area (area outside of the ramp parking area). A clearance is needed for airplanes or airport equipment to be moved (i.e., fueling trucks, emergency vehicles, mowing equipment, personal vehicles). A read-back of the clearance is also required and is recorded for future use if needed. This action confirms with ground control that you have heard and acknowledged the instructions for movement. Likewise, it is imperative for each of us, in every life venture we embark upon, to hear correctly, brief the flight plan before the takeoff roll and then follow the instructions we've heard once airborne.

CHAPTER 11

THE PROMISE

We were somewhere over Mississippi or Louisiana, on our way home from Mexico late in 2008. Pam and I were enjoying a nice ride over scattered clouds. We had spent most of what we had providing meals and other items to children in Mexico. Latin American Ministry was at a critical point. I spent most of my quiet moments petitioning the Lord for help to continue the work, wondering about its future. As we flew along, we passed the occasional fluffy white cloud floating eastward in an otherwise-clear sky. Since I don't remember the exact altitudes I will make an educated guess at them. I would predict we were at 7,000 feet and the clouds were at 6,000. Traveling eastward, it is certain my altitude would have been at an odd thousand feet (i.e. 3, 5, 7, 9, etc.). As was—and is—my custom, I choose the altitude based upon best wind speed and direction. I always want to receive the most help possible from the wind. The faster the wind behind me, the faster the ground passes below me. It was some time past noon moving toward mid afternoon; the sun was at perhaps a 45° angle to the airplane. I looked out as we approached another one of those fluffy white marshmallows hanging in the late summer sky and I saw something that I've only seen a couple of times in the past 18 years. The sun cast the shadow of our airplane onto the cloud, but around the shadow of the plane was a clear and perfectly formed rainbow encircling N30230. I gasped when I saw it. It was there for a few seconds and then it was gone. The shadow that is, but the promise that came with it still burns in my heart today. I felt strongly that I heard the Lord saying to me, "I will take care of you just as I promised I'd do when you bought this airplane. I haven't changed my mind. Don't spend your time worrying about my provision, spend your time using my provision to reach others." That is a paraphrase of what I felt

COCKPIT LESSON

God's not limited by our limits or restricted about our restrictions.

He was speaking to us that day. The memory of that moment has pushed me through some difficult times. There've been some times when we've had more month than money, but there's never been a time that has had more need than need meter. He has been so faithful to us it is difficult to put into words. Here's something else I've learned in the cockpit: God's not limited by our limits or restricted about our restrictions.

This rainbow phenomenon actually has a few names. It's called a glory, or a pilot's bow. It only occurs when the conditions are right (including moisture in the form of clouds or fog and sun). The technical name is anti corona. It is a rare formation which only occurs when the sun is at just the right angle to cast the shadow of the airplane on the mist or the cloud.

A couple of years later we were somewhere over Missouri and I saw that same phenomenon. The only difference was, this time it lasted longer and I had a camera close at hand. I was able to capture a picture of the rainbow around the shadow. I've talked to a few commercial pilots who have also seen a glory.

Through the years that little airplane has been an amazing tool that God placed in our hands. N30230 has safely carried us to destinations in many parts of the US and Mexico. It has carried people and provisions thousands of miles to bless others. I have logged more than 1800 hours behind the controls. If converted to miles, it would be something north of 200,000. In that time two mechanics have made sure we were safe: Doug Vaubel and John Hudson. Both men had one goal in mind, to help us spread the gospel of Jesus Christ to as many people as possible. I've helped on at least a dozen annuals and done owner maintenance between annuals. Another thing I've learned in the cockpit is: Pilots aren't the only ones who make flights successful. There are many components that go into flying, not least of which are provided

COCKPIT LESSON

Pilots aren't the only ones who make flights successful.

by those who never leave the ground. Likewise, I've learned that successful ministry includes people who will never be seen on the stage. They may perform all of their duties far from the luster of the lights and may never hear their voice on air. It's important to remember this: Whether you're serving in a ministry or the one being served, no one is an island and no one can do it alone. If you're the one standing in the light that others see on the platform, it is absolutely critical that you recognize those who are shinning that light. Your calling may be to the masses but your success depends upon those who are called to the trenches to help you.

I find it interesting that such a phenomena be called a *Glory*. For Pam and me that's certainly what it was. It was a moment of glory to remember. Of course God's promises can all be counted as glorious and if He's spoken something to you, it can be believed forever. God's promise to us in the cockpit that day is still a reality. It's been perhaps a dozen years since I've seen the Glory around the plane, yet I know His protection and provision are still there and His unseen hand still guides us. He has never been out of reach for us. Promises from God are not part of our past, they are part of our future. They don't grow old, they grow close.

The *Sky Is The Limit* to what God can do through you, if you avail yourself of Him. Do not allow fear to make decisions for you. Never concede that God-given right. Push back against fear and make your choices and decisions based upon faith instead. If I'd have allowed fear to govern, this book would not have been written, because I would have got out of the airplane on that first flight and never looked back. It was not the fear of flying but the fear of doing it alone. I'm so thankful I didn't get out. Oh, and by the way, let me state for the record, I've never been alone for even one flight. Jesus has been along on every one.

I want to leave you with this final thought: I believe the greatest thing I've learned in the cockpit is:

Every time I leave the ground I defy gravity the right to keep me down.

Even though the law of gravity is working against me, the law of lift, is working for me. Every takeoff is an accomplishment and every landing a victory. I've had some landings when Pam asked, "Did we land or were we shot down?" Getting safe on the ground is more important than making a good impression. Remember, every landing that doesn't damage person or property is a good landing. There will be times in everyone's life when we just have to accept the rough landings and be thankful that nothing but our pride was damaged. To be honest with you, my pride needs a rough landing or two from time to time to keep it in check.

I've enjoyed sharing these pages with you and I pray that this book inspires you to remember that *The Sky's The Limit,* if you're careful to include Him and follow His plans for you.

ABOUT THE AUTHOR

Jim Stockdale is the son of James (Bob) and Virginia Stockdale of Big Sandy, TN. Jim wanted to learn to fly since as a teenager he took a flight with his uncle Junior Hayes in a Cessna 182 over their home in Benton County, TN. By the time Jim turned sixteen, he had accepted a call to preach the gospel. The call he accepted that year has taken Jim around the world. His love for flying has taken him to many places as well. He has worn the hat of: Evangelist, Pastor, Worship Leader, and Missionary. Since accepting the call, in the fall of 1975, Jim has been passionate about whatever he was doing, but he's never strayed too far from his roots and his love of flying. You will find that love in the lines and pages of this book as they translate into practical lessons for the one who longs to learn.

Jim has been married to one woman, Pam since 1980. Jim and Pam prayed for and received two daughters, Kristen Howard, and Brittney Lawley. Benjamin Lawley and Eva Jewel Howard, their two grandchildren, have added even more joy to their lives. Not having sons, Jim is thrilled to call his two Sons-in-Law, Charles Howard, and Kyle Lawley, sons. They are as much a part of his family and future as are his children.

Jim and Pam reside in Dover, TN, only about an hour's drive from his childhood home of Big Sandy. He is President of Latin American Ministry.

From their country home in Stewart, County, TN, he and Pam travel extensively throughout the U.S. and Latin America. Together they preach in churches, conferences, and crusades. They are co-hosts of the talk radio program, Good News. From the home they lovingly refer to as "Paradise Hill," they are leaving a global footprint.

Other Books by The Stockdale's

All titles are available on Amazon.com

Fit To Be Tied - James Stockdale, 2018

Fit To Be Tied Work Book - James Stockdale, 2019

Apto Para Ser Entrenado - James (Santiago) Stockdale, 2019

Apto Para Ser Entrenado, Cuaderno de Trabajo - James

(Santiago) Stockdale, 2019

Snapshots - Pam Stockdale, 2020